# SIMPLE
# MARQUETRY

Designed by Karsten Balsley

# SIMPLE MARQUETRY

Techniques

Projects

Inspirations

## Mike Burton

LARK BOOKS

A Division of Sterling Publishing Co., Inc.
New York

Art Director: Tom Metcalf
Photography: Technical photos by Mike Burton
Project photos by Evan Bracken
Production Assistance: Hannes Charen
Assistant Editor: Veronika Alice Gunter
Proofreader: Kim Catanzarite

Library of Congress Cataloging-in-Publication Data

Burton, Mike.
   Simple Marquetry: techniques, projects, inspirations
   / Mike Burton.
      p.  cm.
   Includes index.
   ISBN 1-57990-171-9
   1. Marquetry. 2. Veneers and veneering. I. Title.

TT192. B87 2001
745.51'2—dc21
                        00-059517
                        CIP


Published by Lark Books, a division of
Sterling Publishing Co., Inc.
387 Park Avenue South, New York, N.Y. 10016

© 2001, Mike Burton

Distributed in Canada by Sterling Publishing,
c/o Canadian Manda Group, One Atlantic Ave., Suite 105
Toronto, Ontario, Canada M6K 3E7

Distributed in the U.K. by Guild of Master Craftsman Publications
Ltd., Castle Place, 166 High Street, Lewes, East Sussex, England
BN7 1XU
Tel: (+ 44) 1273 477374, Fax: (+ 44) 1273 478606, Email:
pubs@thegmcgroup.com, Web: www.gmcpublications.com

Distributed in Australia by Capricorn Link (Australia) Pty Ltd., P.O.
Box 6651, Baulkham Hills, Business Centre
NSW 2153, Australia

If you have questions or comments about this book, please contact:
Lark Books
50 College St.
Asheville, NC 28801
(828) 253-0467

Printed in Hong Kong
ISBN 1-57990-171-9

# Dedication

## To My Grandchildren

*Samuel Ray*

*Alec Michael*

*and*

*Hailey Rose*

# contents

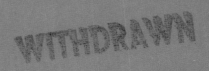

# INTRODUCTION

I have over 40 years of professional woodworking experience, and I have particularly enjoyed the fun and challenge of marquetry. I am pleased to be able to present this exciting craft to you, and it is my hope that you will soon join the ranks of marquetarians everywhere and express your creative visions through this wonderful medium.

Marquetry is the cutting and assembling of a variety of thin woods, called *veneers*, to create often intricate patterns and pictures. Marquetry is generally applied to another object, such as a tray or box, but it can also be used to create a stand-alone picture to hang on the wall. The marquetarian enjoys the rare privilege of knowing and working with beautiful, even glamorous, woods from the four corners of the world. These exotic species are not readily available as lumber, so the more exotic woods are generally beyond the budget of the typical woodworker. However, in veneer form, exotic woods are plentiful and inexpensive.

This wonderful craft can be enjoyed by all, regardless of gender, physical conditioning, or age. My children were cutting pieces of veneer as soon as they could handle knives and fret saws—much to the dismay of my lovely lady who had to bandage the occasional minor cut sometimes inflicted by one of the above mentioned instruments. Unlike other woodworking crafts that require saws, jointers, drill presses, and power sanders, marquetry doesn't demand an investment in expensive tools or machinery. In fact, all the projects I made for this book and all the how-to photos were done at my dining room table. The workbench you see is actually a particleboard cap that fits over my dining table to protect it. I spread a couple of old bed sheets on the floor to protect the carpet and kept the vacuum cleaner nearby. A tidy

**Frank Helvey,** *The Ole' Sourdough.* Narra, carpathian elm burl, maple burl, walnut burl, pearwood, holly, and dyed veneers in various shades. Photo by Edward Reilly

6

workspace is not only more enjoyable, it's safer too. (Anyway, the roar of machinery and the bustle of employees at my shop, are just not conducive to the concentration required for fine detailed work.)

In this book, I'll present a number of different methods for meeting the challenges likely to be encountered by the marquetarian. I encourage you to try any and all of these various methods to determine which is best suited to your project, budget, work environment, and comfort level. What works for one does not necessarily work for all, so try the different approaches and techniques and see what works for *you*. Remember, practice is the key to enjoying any new craft experience; just don't practice on your masterpiece.

**John Russel,** *Frank* (after Frank Lloyd Wright). Photo by Bob Barrett

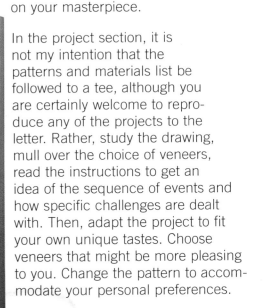

In the project section, it is not my intention that the patterns and materials list be followed to a tee, although you are certainly welcome to reproduce any of the projects to the letter. Rather, study the drawing, mull over the choice of veneers, read the instructions to get an idea of the sequence of events and how specific challenges are dealt with. Then, adapt the project to fit your own unique tastes. Choose veneers that might be more pleasing to you. Change the pattern to accommodate your personal preferences.

And, feel free to modify any technique suggested to accommodate your personal skills.

If you're looking for a little inspiration, visit the Gallery to see some exquisite examples of marquetry mastery. With practice and perseverance, who knows?

Marquetry is a vast stage for personal expression. Enjoy.

8

# MARQUETRY
## HOW TO

Wood Veneers

Cutting and Taping Veneer

Grounds

9

Glues

Methods of Bonding

Finishing

# WOOD VENEER

Strictly speaking, a *veneer* is a thin sheet of a given material. In woodworking terms, a veneer refers to a thin layer of high-quality, often exotic wood that is used to cover a wood of lesser quality. In marquetry, both exotic and common veneers are cut and combined to create exquisitely crafted surface decorations and designs. *Wood* veneer is the traditional marquetry medium, but other thin and delicate materials, such as flat silver wire, mica, stone, and mother-of-pearl, can be beautifully incorporated into many marquetry projects.

Creating finely detailed pictures from wood veneers is much like fine art painting. In fact, marquetry is often described as *painting with wood*.

Just as a painter selects and mixes colors from his or her palette, the marquetarian selects veneers from both native and exotic trees. Just as the painter chooses a particular brush to create a desired texture, so the marquetarian chooses from a myriad of different textures, grains, and hues of veneers. Granted, the marquetarian may have a limited selection of natural colors; but dyes, shading techniques, and finishes greatly enhance creative expression. In addition, veneers provide a certain iridescence, a certain depth, or *fire* unknown to paint.

**Photo 1**

Figure 1

- Oyster shell
- Crotch
- Burl
- Trunk
- Stump
- Butt

## WHERE VENEER COMES FROM

Veneers taken from different parts of the same tree (see figure 1) may have very dissimilar characteristics.

**Photo 2**

*Trunk*. Veneers taken from the trunk and larger limbs have the very familiar grain pattern and texture of sawn lumber. These veneers are the largest, most plentiful, and the least expensive.

Veneer manufacturers use much more than just the trunk of the tree. With conservation on the minds of so many these days, complete utilization of the tree is important. Besides, there are so many beautiful designs within a tree that no part should be discarded.

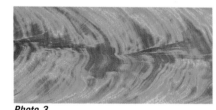

**Photo 3**

*Crotch*. Veneers taken from the crotch of the tree display a unique wavy pattern, caused by the weight concentrated at the base point. In many species, the crotch veneer is quite dark, but it can be bleached and dyed to resemble the ripples in water.

**Photo 4**

*Burls*. Those ugly bulges on the sides of trees (that resemble cancerous growths or large warts) produce surprisingly beautiful veneers. They contain swirling grain and contrasts of color, with designs as wonderful as clouds on a summer's day.

10

Photo 5

*Stump.* The base of the tree, which would otherwise be discarded, contains wavy patterns. The tremendous weight concentrated here compresses and distorts the patterns, making them quite similar to those found higher up the tree. The rippled appearance of stump wood resembles some exotic species.

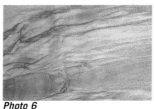
Photo 6

*Buttress.* Farther down are the growths that resemble roots. This area produces veneers that resemble burls.

Photo 7

*Oyster shell.* Smaller limbs are often considered for veneer. These are cut across their length to produce oyster shell veneer. These veneers display the annular (or ring) pattern of the limb and are most dramatic when taken from oval or axially distorted growths.

## HOW VENEER IS TAKEN FROM THE TREE

Throughout the ages, veneers have been taken from trees by riving, splitting, sawing, and slicing. Today, veneers that are too hard to cut other ways are still sawn from the log. However, sawing is wasteful because the *kerf* (the width of material that a saw blade removes as it cuts) is often wider than the thickness of the actual veneer being cut. Most of the veneers you will encounter are sliced with a huge knife, measuring 15 feet (4.5 m) or more. Needless to say, that knife is attached to some very impressive, hydraulically operated, heavy-duty machinery.

Before sawing or slicing, the logs must be prepared. First the bark is removed, and then the logs are checked with a metal detector for hidden

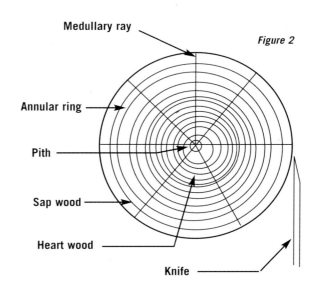
Figure 2

Medullary ray
Annular ring
Pith
Sap wood
Heart wood
Knife

and unwanted *surprises.* Pieces of fence, nails from old campsites, even soft, lead bullets, can damage the knife. (And small nicks in the knife produce veneers that require more sanding.) After the metal detector stage, the logs may be halved or quartered. They may even be squared up into timbers for easy machine mounting. Veneers from squared timbers are uniform in width and require no trimming. The logs are then soaked in hot water, or steamed to soften. This is a very important step, as the softness and pliability of wood increases continually as the temperature is raised to 250 ° F (121° C).

*11*

## SLICING TECHNIQUES

A variety of slicing machines and techniques are used to produce different patterns.(see figure 2). Here are some of the more popular techniques:

Photo 8

*Plain sliced.* If the knife begins slicing on the edge of the log, a veneer pattern called *plain sliced* will result. This will produce the familiar *flame* pattern seen in sawn lumber.

Photo 9

*Rift.* As slicing continues and slices are taken from the log not quite parallel with the medullar rays, a pattern called rift develops.

Photo 10

*Quartered.* Finally, slices taken parallel with the medullar rays, or perpendicular to the rings of the log produce a pattern called *quartered*, because the log is actually quartered before it is mounted on the slicing machine. Here, the ray pattern of the log will be dramatically displayed on the face of the veneer.

*Rotary slicing.* The log may also be mounted on a lathe. See figure 3. As the log is rotated, the knife is advanced, producing a continuous slice of veneer. The flame pattern that results is very bold and often rather unattractive. This process is quick and inexpensive, and most rotary-sliced veneers wind up in the cores of plywood. Of course, some patterns, such as birds-eye maple, can only be obtained by rotary slicing. Another rotary machine produces slices with *a moderate* flame pattern—bolder than plain slicing, but not as dramatic as rotary slicing. See figure 4. This technique has the advantage of producing wider veneers than plain slicing.

There are many variations of the techniques mentioned above. The craft of veneer slicing is rather

**12**

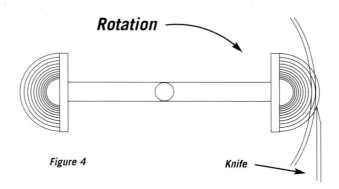

**Rotation**

Figure 4        Knife

involved. What matters most to the marquetarian is what ends up on the shelf of the supplier. Now you know how veneer patterns came to be.

# VENEER AVAILABILITY

Veneer is available in several forms. Your choice will depend on your specific project needs, your budget, and species selection.

## RAW VENEER

After the veneers have been sliced, they are dried and stacked in the order they were taken from the log. They may undergo some edge trimming to make for easier handling. Some veneers are very neat and of uniform width. Others will still have the ragged outline of the tree from which they were cut. These are referred to as *raw* veneers. In this raw condition, the selection of species will be the greatest and the cost will be least.

## PAPER-BACKED VENEERS

Several manufacturers supply a limited number of species of veneers bonded to a paper backing, as shown in photo 11. Slices may be joined together to form sheets as large as 48 x 96 inches (123 x 240 cm). The paper backing substantially strengthens the veneers and makes them easier to use. The price of paper-backed veneer will usually

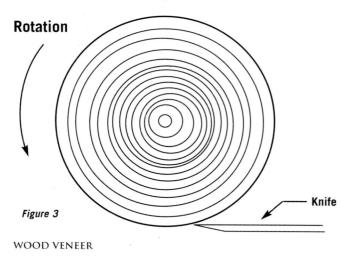

**Rotation**

Figure 3        Knife

be more than raw veneer. In addition, the smallest piece of paper-backed readily available is 18 x 96 inches (46 x 240 cm). If you plan a small project using five different species, you will make quite an investment and have a lot left over.

## PEEL-AND-STICK

Veneers are now available with an incorporated pressure-sensitive adhesive. Ah, the convenience! No messy glue to handle. Ah, the ease! Just cut the veneer to fit, peel off the protective backing paper, and stick in place. Ah, the cost! The problem is you will find only a limited selection of species and an unreliable pressure-sensitive adhe-

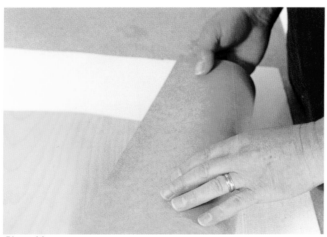

**Photo 11**

sive. (If you must use a peel-and-stick veneer, let me give you a tip from my days as a floor-covering installer: Prepare your ground material with a very thin coat of contact cement. This will ensure that you have adhesive-compatible surfaces. If you still have trouble, apply heat from a household iron that is quite warm to the touch.)

# SPECIAL CONSIDERATIONS

Wood veneer has its quirks and peculiarities, just like any other material. Let's consider a few you're likely to encounter and learn how to successfully deal with them.

## OILS AND RESINS

Several kinds of veneer contain oils and resins that can present challenges. For example, teak and rosewoods are quite oily. Pine and other softwoods are likely to have pitch pockets. In many cases, these oils and resins inhibit the actions of the bonding adhesive. More often, they will slow or completely prevent the drying of some finishing products. A good test for the presence of oils and resins is to place the suspect veneer on a clean piece of white paper and heat it with a household iron set on medium heat. If the veneer sticks to the paper or there is a "grease spot" left, you'll want to scrub down the veneer using a generous amount of a solvent, such as acetone, MEK, or lacquer thinner. (NOTE: These are flammable solvents. There are certain health risks involved in their use; be sure to read and understand all of the cautions on the container.) Some manufacturers even suggest soaking the veneer in the solvent, but I've never had to go that far.

## MINERAL DEPOSITS

To sustain life, a tree draws water from the soil. This water may contain dissolved minerals. In most cases these minerals will only alter the color of the wood, or they will go completely unnoticed. In other cases, they will form rock- hard deposits within the tree. The dark streaks in teak are particularly offensive. How the slicing knife survives these deposits, I'll never know. Should you discover that your cutting tools become dull very quickly, or if you discover nicks in your blades, it is very possible you are cutting veneers with significant (although not pronounced) mineral deposits.

## LIGHTFASTNESS

Over time, the natural colors of veneers can change rather dramatically. Mahogany and cherry darken, the purple cast of walnut fades to a warm brown, and oak yellows. That wonderful green in

**13**

poplar—the only green for the palette—quickly turns brown. Some of these changes are caused by exposure to air, but more often they are caused by exposure to ultraviolet light.

When your project is still in the planning stages, test the pieces of veneer you will be using by taping a piece of cardboard or heavy paper over a portion of each and exposing them to sunlight for a few weeks. Remove the cardboard and observe how much the veneer has changed color, as shown in photos 12a to 12d. If the veneers still meet your color requirements, proceed with your project. If not, you will have to make other arrangements. Wha' other arrangements? Many homes and buildings now incorporate UV-inhibiting glass in all windows. If you don't have the advantage of protective windows, consider placing UV-inhibiting glass over your project.

12 a

Walnut

12 b

Cedar

12 c

RoseWood

Dyeing is another possibility. One major manufacture of cherry furniture routinely bleaches its product as a first step in finishing. The color is then replaced with dye and pigment colors that are far more lightfast than the natural color of the cherry. (I must say their bleached-and-dyed product does not have the subtle tones and contrasts of untreated cherry, but a floral arrangement shading the center of a dining table won't leave a light spot.)

OAK

12 d

Another option is to use UV-inhibiting varnish in your finishing process. Most readily available are the polyurethane varnishes with UV-inhibitor.

Some lacquers have UV-inhibitor, but these are industrial products and not available to the general public. Should you decide to go this route, run some tests by coating small pieces of the veneer you intend to use with the varnish. Cover a portion with cardboard as described above and expose the veneer to sunlight. Though not as protective as the glass, UV-inhibiting varnish may work for the veneer you are using.

At the risk of sounding foolish, let me share one more option. Add a tiny bit of pearl essence to clear coat finishes to help prevent fading. Pearl essence is made from ground pearls and is typically used as an automotive finish. Look for it in your local automotive supply store. I discovered this technique while doing some touch-up work. I often add pearl to my patches to simulate the iridescence of wood. I find that the spots colored with the pearl hold their tone and hue far better than those without the pearl.

If your color choice is critical, be sure to experiment with the veneers you intend to use.

## DIFFERENT THICKNESSES

Some suppliers say their raw veneer is between $\frac{1}{28}$ and $\frac{1}{32}$ inch (.9 and .8 mm) thick. But I'm here to tell you that it ain't necessarily so. Different countries have different standards for slicing veneer. Some mills are better equipped than others, and some woods can only be sliced so thin. Some manufacturers sand their veneers, and while these are wonderful to work with, they are substantially thinner than $\frac{1}{32}$ inch (.8 mm).

What does all this mean to the marquetarian? A lot of scraping or sanding. It also means that some added care is needed in the bonding process—we'll discuss that later. If you are using a mix of raw and paper-back veneers, it also means that you could very easily sand through the veneer into the paper backing, since the veneer is often thinner than the backing. Be aware of the different thicknesses of the materials you are using before

14

you start the project. In some cases, you may need to adjust the thickness of some of your veneers.

A good way to equalize your veneers is to fasten two scrap strips of your thinnest veneers to a working surface with rubber cement. Then, with a sanding block or cabinet scraper, work on the thicker veneer until the block or scraper begins to make contact with or kiss the thin strips (photo 13).

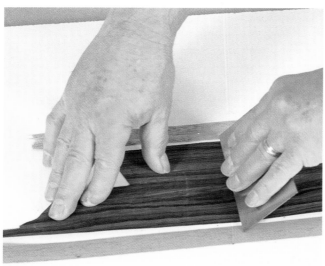

Photo 13

# ATTENDING TO DEFECT AND DAMAGE

Veneers are not perfect. They shrink substantially as they dry and this can lead to *end checks*, or *voids*, in the ends that will not fit back together without deforming the sheet. If you can plan your cutting so that any defects wind up in the waste, by all means do so. Veneer is not nearly as expensive as the time it takes to fiddle with it. But in cases where you must fiddle...

## COMPRESSION

As veneer is sliced, it curves away from the knife much the same way shavings leave a hand plane. This causes the side nearest the log to stretch

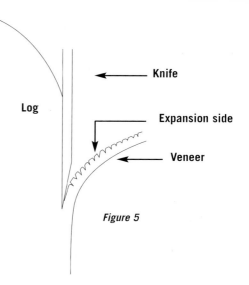

Figure 5

while the opposite side is forced to compress. See figure 5. Many woods can be compressed up to 20 percent without failure. But most woods, when caused to stretch over 7 percent, will *check*. That is, the fibers will be torn from each other, as in photo 14. The other side will be very smooth, sometimes having a glossy appearance, as in photo 15. Checking can be so severe that it creates

Photo 14

**15**

a rough, unattractive texture. Make this rough, checked side the backside of your marquetry project. This is the side you'll bond, or glue. The smooth, shiny side is the front and referred to as the *face*—this is the side you show the world.

Photo 15

To determine which side is which, bend the edges of the sheet of veneer toward you.

If the veneer bends freely, you are looking at the face (see photo 16). If the veneer offers considerable resistance—you may even hear some cracking—you are looking at the checked (or back) side.

It's a good idea to mark the checked side with chalk, so you don't display it in your masterpiece. If, however, the checked side winds up smiling at you after you've bonded the piece, you will have to sand to the approximate center of the piece to remove the checks.

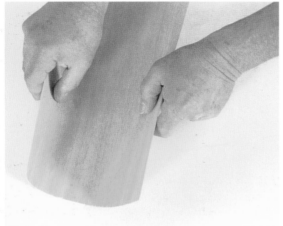

**Photo 16**

## HOLES

Burls are notorious for having holes. These appear where there was a brittle, knotlike structure that fell out after the veneer dried. Even if these areas are intact when you unpack your burl veneers, the brittle areas may fall out when you attempt to flatten it.

In most cases these structures are dark and have little character or iridescence, so let them fall. If the holes are quite small, you may fill them with putty and restore their color in the finishing process. If the holes are large, the putty and color will look like a blob of nonwood. You will have to insert a patch into these. Patching consists of cutting away any dark, brittle structure and inserting a piece of veneer similar in character to the surrounding area. (Make your cut irregularly shaped, and your patch will barely be noticeable.)

## END CHECKS

As a slice of veneer dries, it often checks on the end. Sometimes the check was in the log from which the veneer was sliced (see photo 17). It's always best to cut around checks, but if that's not possible, first examine the edges of the check. If they are dark, the check was probably present in the log and picked up some contamination as it was dragged through the forest or jungle. In this case, the dark edges need to be cut away and a wedge-shaped piece of veneer with similar grain and texture inserted. The same applies if the check is much wider than 1/4 inch (6 mm).

*Photo 17*

If the check is small, it is possible to pull it together and tape it. This will, of course, cause the end of the veneer to *cup*—just like you would cup your hand—but this cupping can be flattened using a household iron. (See Flattening Veneer on page 17 for more information.)

## SPLITS AND TEARS

Often you will unpack a shipment of veneer that has splits on the ends or tears on the jagged edges. These are a result of rough handling. Unlike checks, when these are pulled back together, they will fit perfectly without distorting the sheet. It's a good idea to tape these splits and tears to keep them from getting worse. I routinely tape the ends of very fragile veneers to prevent splitting from my own rough handling. Since my tape may wind up in the *glue line*—the bonding glue between the back of the veneer and the ground material—I use the thin perforated type of veneer tape. (It's best that no tape is left in the glue line, but the thin, perforated type is acceptable. See Taping Veneers on page 41 for more information.)

# FLATTENING VENEER

**Photo 18**

Raw veneers do not always come in a completely flat condition; this is especially true of patterned slices—burls, crotches, stump, etc. (see photo 18). In many cases the veneers are so wrinkled that trying to hold them flat for marking and cutting breaks them. With these wrinkled slices, flattening is an important first step.

**Photo 19**

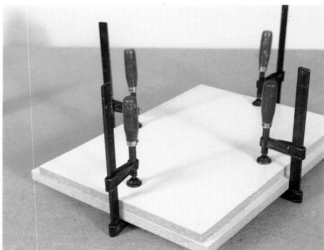

**Photo 20**

## USING A HOUSEHOLD IRON

Small pieces may be flattened easily with an iron and spray bottle, just as you would iron clothes, but use a hard surface, instead of a padded ironing board. See photo 19. Mist both sides of the veneer with clean water and allow it to soak in for a few minutes. Then, with an iron set on medium heat, begin ironing without exerting any pressure. The heat from the iron will help soften the veneer and make it pliable. As the veneer warms, increase the pressure on the iron and turn the veneer frequently. Continue ironing until the veneer is flat and dry.

You can also do this with a steam iron. Pass the steam jets of the iron over both sides of the veneer and increase your pressure on the iron. Then turn off the steam and continue ironing until the veneer is flat. Remember to turn the veneer frequently.

## USING A PRESS (WITH WATER, GLYCERIN, AND ALCOHOL)

One major veneer supplier recommends spraying veneers generously with a mixture of 8 ounces. (224 g) glycerin, 8 ounces (224 g) alcohol, and enough water to make 1 gallon (3.8 L). Then place the veneers in a press. Apply pressure to the press gently and slowly until the veneers are flat.

Don't be discouraged by that word "press." A press can consist of a couple of pieces of ¾-inch (1.9 cm) particleboard, plywood, or Medium Density Fiberboard (MDF), and a few clamps. I'm very partial to the coated particleboard used by kitchen cabinet manufacturers because the coating keeps the liquid from swelling and distorting the particleboard. (See photo 20.)

Pay careful attention to the words "gently" and "slowly." Initially, tighten the clamps just enough to keep them from falling off. Every few minutes snug them down a little more. It may take 30 minutes to flatten the veneer completely. If you don't have glycerin or alcohol on hand, water alone will work, but not as well.

Photo 21

Photo 22

## STEAM

Depending on the size of your veneers and your culinary equipment, you can steam them flat in your kitchen. I place small pieces on a cooling rack in a large roasting pan with about 1 inch (2.5 cm) boiling water in the bottom as shown in photo 21. Covering the pan concentrates the steam, and after about 10 minutes, the veneer is as limp as a wet dishrag. Well, not quite that limp, but it is very pliable. After steaming, quickly place the veneer in your pressing device. Tighten it quickly and let it set for about 15 minutes, until the veneer is cool.

## DRYING AND STORING VENEER

If you used water or steam to flatten your veneers, they will have to be dried before you can use them. You can place the veneers in a press with blotter paper or newspaper between them. Anything that will absorb the moisture will work— even cloth. (Never use fresh newspaper, as the uncured ink can transfer to the veneers, especially if  was alcohol used in the flattening solution.) Whatever absorbent material you choose to put between the veneers, it must be changed periodi-

cally until the veneer is thoroughly dry. If you used steam, you might get away with only one change.

When I was a child, my job was to change the newspaper on the bottom of the birdcage and beneath the cat's box. One year for Lent, I gave up birds, cats, and changing newspaper. It became one of those good Lenten habits that has remained to this day. So when I dry veneers, I place them between sheets of a product called *single side*. See photo 22. This is corrugated cardboard with a single side of smooth paper. It's available from packing and shipping suppliers. I position it so the corrugations all run in the same direction, and I situate a small fan to blow air through them. In my climate, veneers flattened with steam will dry overnight. Those flattened with water take a couple of days, and I don't ever have to change the newspaper.

Flattened, dry veneers have a tendency to wrinkle again with time and changing humidity conditions. To prevent this, I store my flattened veneers flat on a shelf between pieces of cardboard, covered with a piece of particleboard.

## STRENGTHENING VENEER

Veneers are quite fragile. Many will not readily yield to the fine detailed cutting required for marquetry projects, but don't let the challenges of the medium compromise your art. There are several ways to strengthen veneers, permitting them to yield to your designs.

## SIZING

Applying a thin coat of glue (called *sizing*) to the back side of the veneer will impart considerable strength. This is not quite as simple as it sounds, since the moisture in the glue also causes the veneer to curl almost immediately. To prevent this, first mist the face side with water, as shown in photo 23. This will equalize the moisture content of both sides and help the veneer remain reasonably flat. Then, coat the backside with white, yellow, or liquid hide glue thinned one part water to two parts glue, as shown in photo 24. Once the glue has set up a bit—most of the opaque areas will have disappeared—place the veneers between layers of singleside. To prevent the fresh glue from sticking to the singleside, place a layer of fiberglass window screen above and below the veneer, as shown in photo 25.

## REINFORCING WITH PAPER TAPE

Placing gummed, paper veneer-tape over potential trouble spots is another good way to strengthen veneer. The object is not to cover the whole veneer, but just the outline of the shape you intend to cut, especially those areas that may tear out or chip during cutting, as shown in photo 26. You may have to trace your pattern lightly onto the veneer so you know where to position the tape, then trace it again, over the tape. Yes, it's an extra step, but well worth it. See Taping Veneers on page 41 for more information.

## BONDING TO PAPER

Another way to strengthen veneer is to bond it to paper—essentially making your own paper-back product. If you are partial to working with paper-back veneers, learning to bond your own will increase the species in your palette many times over. Almost any clean paper will work, but I've always been partial to fine tissue paper, as it has a

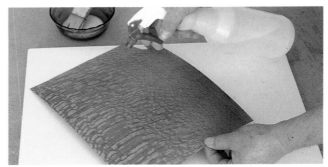

**Photo 23**

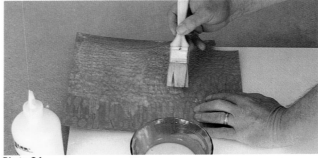

**Photo 24**

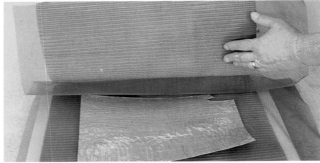

**Photo 25**

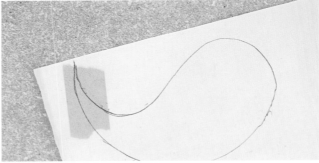

**Photo 26**

minimum effect on the thickness of the veneer. To bond the tissue, first mist the face side of the veneer with water, then brush the glue on the backside and gently place the tissue on the glue. I use liquid hide glue (you can also use white or yellow poly vinyl acetate [PVA] glue) thinned one part water to two parts glue. Work the tissue down with a stiff brush and set the assembly to dry between pieces of single side and fiberglass screen.

# COLORING VENEER

One of the drawbacks to "painting" with natural veneers is the limited colors at your disposal. However, veneers may be colored—even shaded for depth and definition—to your wishes, making the selection very broad.

## BLEACHING

(NOTE: All bleaches are hazardous chemicals and dangerous to work with. Never permit bleaching solutions to directly contact your skin. Rubber gloves and long sleeve shirts are a must. Goggles or at least safety glasses should be worn when working with bleach. Bleaches often release toxic fumes so if you have a respirator, use it. If you don't have a respirator, work in a well-ventilated area—outdoors on a breezy day is best. Different solutions have different characteristics, so be sure to read and understand all cautions printed on the labels.)

The color of veneer may be lightened or removed completely with bleach. Here are several good bleaching options.

*Wood-bleach kits.* These commercially prepared, three-part systems work well on almost all species. The *bleach* is applied to the veneer and allowed to penetrate for a time. Then, a second solution—the *activator*—is applied; this solution dramatically speeds the action of the bleach. After the bleach-

ing action is complete, a third solution—the *neutralizer*—is applied to prevent further chemical action that may deteriorate the veneer. The instructions supplied with the bleaching kit provide all the necessary timings. I can't say it too many times—read and understand all of the directions on the label. I highly recommend wood-bleach kits because they work the best overall.

*Chlorine bleach.* The kind used in your laundry will bleach some species. Apply the bleach full strength or soak the veneer in a large plastic container filled with bleach. Make sure your container has a tight-fitting lid—the fumes are very unpleasant and are highly toxic in concentration. The action of chlorine bleach on some species is quite slow; it may take several hours or overnight soaking to completely work. The right side of the piece of walnut in photo 27 was soaked in a plastic cup containing $\frac{1}{2}$ inch (1.3 cm) of chlorine bleach for about 1 hour. The left side was left in the bleach overnight. It is very white, but it's also partially disintegrated. Be careful with bleach, and monitor it closely.

**Photo 27**

The bleaching action may be speeded by letting it soak into the wood for 5 to 20 minutes, then applying a heavy coat of 3 percent hydrogen-peroxide—sold in pharmacies as disinfectant. The hydrogen peroxide adds needed oxygen for the bleaching action and is reasonably safe to work with. Once the bleaching action is complete, neutralize it by applying a generous amount of vinegar and rinse thoroughly with water.

*Peroxide hair bleach.* Yes, the same stuff used to make blondes out of brunettes will remove the color from some woods. After reading all cautions on the container, use the solution full strength and keep the veneer wetted with solution until the desired effect is achieved. Once the veneer is bleached, rinse thoroughly with water to remove any residues. No neutralizer is necessary.

*Oxalic acid.* This crystalline substance is available from your local pharmacist and is a time-honored chemical used for bleaching wood. (Some paint stores offer an oxalic acid solution for restoring color to redwood and cedar decks.) Add the crystals to water at the rate of 1 ounce per pint (28 g to .47L). Like chlorine, oxalic acid is *slow.* You may need to keep the veneer wet with the solution for several hours or, in some cases, soak it overnight.

No matter what bleach you use, remember that heat speeds up the bleaching action; work in a warm but well-ventilated area. Experiment with scraps of veneer before applying any bleaching solution to your project pieces. After the test pieces are dry, be sure to scrape or sand them lightly. This will let you know just how deeply the veneer has been bleached and give you an idea how much (or little) sanding you can get away with.

## DYEING

Though dyed veneers may be purchased, the color assortment is rather small and tends to be vivid (and therefore best used in border arrangements). If you desire more subtle hues, you will want to do your own dyeing. Here are the two most popular methods of dyeing veneer.

*Aniline dyes.* I've found that these work best for dyeing veneer. Use the products that are blended with alcohol or lacquer thinner, they won't wrinkle your veneer the way water-based dyes will. You must experiment to determine the strength of the dye that will produce the color you want. Dipping small pieces of veneer into various strengths of the dye for a few minutes will often give you a good indication of the final color. Although the dyed veneer will lighten substantially as it dries, the finishing medium will usually return the veneer to its approximate wet color. If color is critical, it's a good idea to carry the test piece through the whole process of dyeing, drying, and finishing.

Dye should completely penetrate the veneer. If the dye is only on the surface, and you end up having to sand, you will remove the dyed surface and be back to what you started with. That's why the veneer must be soaked in the dye at least overnight. Sometimes it may take days. Soft-textured veneers—poplar, alder, pine, for example—will dye much easier than hard-textured veneers—such as birch, maple, and hickory. To test for complete penetration, wipe off the sample and cut into the heart of it to see if the dye has penetrated completely. See photo 28. You'll note that in the photo, it has not.

Dyeing hard-textured, open-grain veneers such as oak, ash, and hickory, will produce interesting effects. The dye will penetrate the porous areas very well but will penetrate the solid areas very little. After a light sanding, the porous areas will retain the color of the dye, while the solid areas will remain the original color of the veneer. See photo 29. This effect can be used quite creatively in many marquetry projects.

**Photo 28**

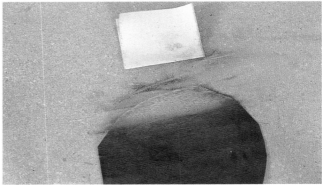

**Photo 29**

*Fabric dyes.* These dyes are available at your local variety or grocery store. They are all water-soluble and reasonably safe. However, at room temperature, they may take weeks to completely penetrate. The action can be speeded up by adding alcohol at the rate of 1 part alcohol to 2 parts water. One tablespoon (15 mL) of glycerin to 1 quart (.95 L) dye will also be helpful. *Liquid* dye concentrates work better than the *powdered* types. Be sure to read all cautions on the package, and in the case of the powered dye concentrates, omit the salt when mixing.

Use a plastic container to immerse the veneer in the dye mixture, as shown in photo 30. Keep the veneer off the bottom of the container, and if you are dyeing several pieces, keep them separated. I use some old stainless-steel flatware for the purpose; it's impervious to the dye.

To speed the action of fabric dye, you can heat it. Omit the alcohol and glycerin, and use a porcelain-lined pan. The dye should be kept hot, but not boiling. The pine veneer in photo 31 took eight hours to completely penetrate. As with the aniline dyes, some experimentation is in order.

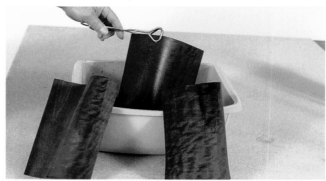
**Photo 30**

**Photo 31**

## SHADING AND HIGHLIGHTING

Shade and highlight can add depth to many marquetry projects; in fact, shade and highlight are a must for many projects. The petals of a flower, the leaves of a tree, even the feathers of a bird will be lifeless if cut from the same species without some shade or highlight. Though some shade or highlight may be added in the finishing process with a brush, dye, and a gentle touch, other techniques may be used on individual pieces while the project is in progress.

## SAND SHADING

The time-honored technique of shading veneers is to use hot *sand*. The intensity of shading depends on the temperature of the sand and the length of time the veneer is exposed to it.

Use a steel pan to hold the sand; never use aluminum. (It's possible to overheat aluminum to the point of toxicity.) You'll find that a steel bread pan will work very well.

Although any fine sand will work, I highly recommend granite sand as opposed to silica or white sand. The dust produced from handling the silica sand can be quite harmful. Fill your pan to a depth of at least 1 to 2 inches (2.5 to 5 cm). You will also need some scraps of veneer to experiment with. A timer or clock that shows seconds and a notebook will also be helpful. The first time you heat the sand, do so in a well-ventilated room.

**22**

You never know what contaminates might be in the sand and, as these burn off, unpleasant (even toxic) fumes may be released. If you have a camp stove, work outdoors the first time, or place the pan and sand in the barbecue coals after the steaks are cooked.

Place the pan on a heat source set at medium high. If the pan is substantially larger than the heating element, you will have to move the pan about to heat the sand evenly. After about 15 minutes, slide a test piece of veneer vertically into the sand. Keep the edge of the veneer just off the bottom of the pan. After 10 seconds, withdraw the test piece and evaluate the results. You will note the edge of the veneer that was immersed deepest is the darkest, and the shade decreases as the veneer was exposed to the cooler sand on top, as seen in photo 32. Now, make a note of the temperature settings and the time. You may even wish to jot the information on the test piece itself. Try different times and different heat settings; get a feel for the technique. You will find that different species shade differently; soft-textured woods darken far more quickly than hard-textured woods.

You will also find that heating the sand to a very high temperature will shade the edge quite darkly, leaving material away from the edge shaded very little. Reducing the temperature and extending the time, you'll find that the veneer is shaded lightly farther into the piece.

When woking with curved edges, shape the sand to conform to the edge being shaded; for convex edges, scoop some sand from the center of the pan, as shown in photo 33; for those concave edges, build a mound of sand in the center, as shown in photo 34. You can even shade different portions of an edge to different degrees by shaping the sand. To shade an area that can't be immersed, simply sprinkle hot sand on that portion, as shown in photo 35. Remember that sand taken from the bottom of the pan will work faster than the cooler sand on top.

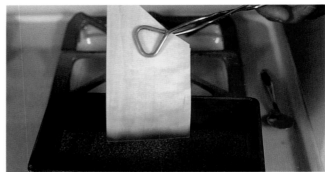
Photo 32

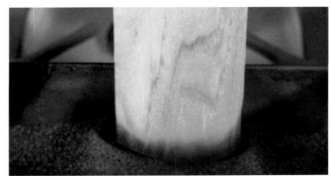
Photo 33

Photo 34

Photo 35

23

When you only have a piece or two to shade, heating the sand will seem a complete nuisance. In these instances I use a propane torch. Obviously, even the low flame of a torch can set the veneer on fire immediately, but if the veneer is passed *quickly* through the flame several times, good results can be obtained. Don't be tempted to regulate the heat by holding the veneer too far from the flame. At a distance of more than about 4 inches (10 cm), air currents deflect the flame in a rather unreliable manner. Simply pass the veneer through the flame about 2 inches (5 cm) beyond the torch head. Regulate the shading by the number of passes and the speed of each pass.

One more heat source worthy of mention is the wood burner (or pyro-pencil). A soldering iron also can be used. The body of the device may be used to darken areas around edges. I've found that the best way to do this is to hold the veneer on the edge of the work surface (see photo 36), and roll the body of the wood burner along the edge. Lean the tool toward or away from the veneer slightly to vary the shadow. The tip can be used for creating dark delicate lines, as shown in photo 37. With a delicate touch, you can also use the tip for light shading, as seen in photo 38. Don't try to create the shade in a single pass. Rather, make several passes, imagining that the tip is an airplane landing then taking off.

## HIGHLIGHTING WITH BLEACH

What do you do when you want to lighten an area? Apply bleach with a fine brush or cotton swab (see photo 39). When the desired highlight has been achieved, neutralize the area with vinegar. If the bleaching action seems to take forever—place a wad of bleach-saturated tissue over the area and check it periodically.

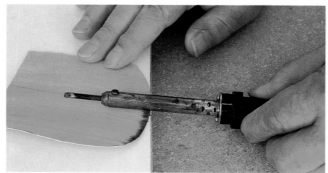
*Photo 36*

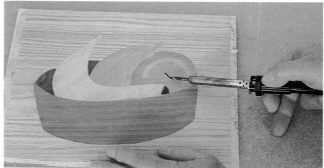
*Photo 37*

*Photo 38*

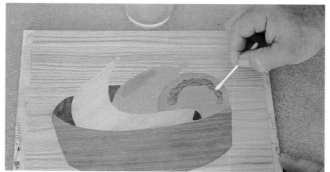
*Photo 39*

24

## JOINING VENEERS

A time will come when you'll need a piece of veneer wider than what you have in stock. Here's what you do: Cut your sheets of veneer to the lengths required, as shown in photo 40. (To avoid confusion, I make a chalk mark down the side of each veneer to indicate grain direction.) Trim any irregular edges (photo 41). Adjustments to your trimming can be made with a sandpaper-covered block (photo 42). Now, tack the joint together with several short pieces of tape across it, then run a continuous piece down the full length. For maximum strength, set the tape with an iron, as shown in photo 43.

## WORKING WITH PATTERNS

Before you make a marquetry project, you need to have a picture or design to work from. This picture is referred to as the *pattern*. Generally, a black-and-white line drawing of a picture or geometric design is used as a pattern. You can trace a picture, or create something on your computer, use a copy machine to make a black-and-white image of a color photograph you may like, or use one of the project patterns at the end of this book.

Once you've selected a design and have modified it to suit your tastes, you might need to reduce or enlarge it to fit your project specifications. Take your drawing or tracing to your local copy/print shop. Use the laser copy machine to reproduce your image in the appropriate size. Some copy machines will even make a mirror image so you can mark your veneers from the back if you choose. Take your laser copies home and warm your iron to about medium high.

**Photo 40**

**Photo 41**

**Photo 42**

**Photo 43**

**25**

The ink on the copy was transferred *to* the paper through a heat process. It may also be transferred *from* the paper with heat. Place the paper face down on the veneer you need to mark and apply heat from the iron to the backside of the paper. If you will be marking a number of different species with the same pattern, make a bunch of copies because the ink is only good for one or two transfers. The transferred line will be light, especially on coarse-textured woods, as seen in photo 44, but it will be accurate. This won't work with an inkjet printer. If you don't have access to a laser copy machine, you can transfer your pattern to your veneers using tracing and carbon paper with a very sharp pencil, or transfer paper (see photo 45). If you need a mirror image, simply run a pencil around your pattern as it rests on a piece of transfer paper with the transfer side up, as shown in photo 46.

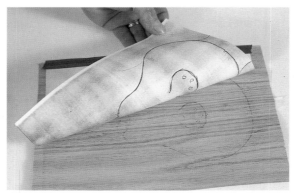
*Photo 44*

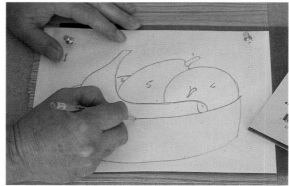
*Photo 45*

## VENEERS OTHER THAN WOOD

Veneers other than wood can enhance many projects. Browse supply catalogues, and let your imagination run wild. Imagine a devil with eyes of mother-of-pearl or abalone shell. Imagine the same devil with real metal prongs on his fork. Give him a collar of ivory. You can use the real thing or one of the many acetate imitations available today. I used one of these in the CD cabinet project on page 82.

Many of these products will have to be used as inlays—inserted into the project after bonding—because the wood veneer bonding adhesive may not adhere to the accent materials. Your supplier can advise you. I bonded the CD door with yellow glue and it seemed to stick well to the imitation mother-of-pearl, which I first scuffed with course sandpaper. Should the pearl come loose in the future, I'll pop the pieces out and bond them with cyanoacrylate or CA. (See page 52 for more information on CA.)

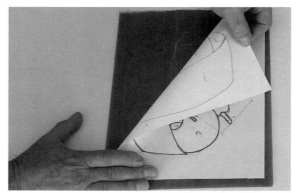
*Photo 46*

26

We've discussed where veneer comes from and the different forms that are available. We've examined some of the special considerations and defects that are inherent with veneers. We've learned a variety of ways to flatten, dry, strengthen, color, and join veneers. I hope that you're not only gaining an understanding of the medium, but an appreciation of the artistry. I mentioned eariler that marquetry is often described as painting with wood. Take a close look at the following examples and you'll see just what I mean.

**Hanya Kandlis,** *Lady on the Bridge.* Walnut crotch, oak, holly, carpathian elm burl, dyed holly, mahogany, ash, mother-of-pearl. Photo by Rob Ratkowski

**Karsten Balsley,** *Haloed Cross Box and Angel Box.* Iron wood, sterling silver, mother-of-pearl, brass, walnut, steamed Swiss pear, moradillo, curly maple, and holly. Photo by artist

**T. Breeze Verdant,** *Warmoth Electric Guitar.* Maple, rosewood, bubinga, and tulipwood. Photo by Jeff Baird

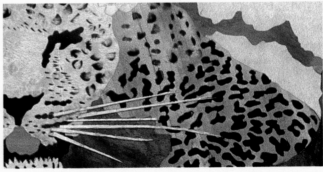

**Frank Helvey,** *Nap Time on the Serengeti (detail).* Maple, walnut crotch, satinwood, dyed black and dark pearwood. Photo by Edward Reilly

# CUTTING AND TAPING VENEER

In marquetry, there are a variety of cutting tools and techniques used. The two basic cutting tools are the knife and the saw. Each has advantages and disadvantages. Most people tend to be more comfortable with knives, but for cutting curves and turns, it's tough to beat a saw. Try all the different tools and see what you're most comfortable using. Become familiar with all the different cutting techniques. This knowledge will not only make you a well-rounded marquetarian, it will allow you to approach any project with confidence.

## CUTTING SURFACE

Before you do any knife cutting, it's important to have a stable, suitable cutting surface. Don't cut directly on top of your work surface. It will be destroyed by repeated small cuts. Further, many work surfaces will soon dull the tip of the knife blade you're using. Cover your work surface with something that's inexpensive, disposable, and won't dull the blade. I highly recommend poster board. Those boxes from the bakery work very well, as do gift boxes. (I'm especially fond of the boxes that protect all of those un-cooked pizzas I buy.)

## TOOLS

There are just a few tools and accessories a marquetarian needs. Treat your tools, knives, and saws with care and you will enjoy long-lasting performance.

## STRAIGHTEDGES AND OTHER GUIDES

If you're going to create your own marquetry patterns, you'll want to invest in a few drawing guides. Although it's said that there are no straight lines in art, I'll be willing to bet you'll need a straight line in some marquetry project. Don't try to make these lines freehand...it's nearly impossible!

You need a straightedge that's wide enough to hold firmly without your fingers hanging over the edge. (If I banked money each time I cut a finger using a narrow straightedge, I'd have retired years ago.) How wide is wide enough? At least 2 inches (5 cm). A plastic see-through straightedge is especially helpful—it allows you to see the grain pattern of the material you're cutting.

I also use a French curve extensively (see photo 1). For cutting small and medium circles, I use a drawing template from the craft store. When I need to cut a large number of pieces a particular shape, I make my own template. I cut mine from 1/8-inch (3 mm) plastic scraps that I get from my glass supplier. For large circles, I cut the plastic with a hole saw or fly cutter, and for irregular shapes, I use a fret saw or band saw.

*Photo 1*

# KNIVES

(NOTE: Knives cut fingers easier than they cut veneer...never place your fingers in the path of the blade. Moreover, always work with sharp knives— they require less force to use, so the prospect of an accident is minimized. Should you cut yourself, attend to it immediately. Your finger will heal, but bloodstains on a project need special attention. Dab stains on veneer with 3 percent hydrogen peroxide.)

The one marquetry skill that you need to sharpen is the ability to cut accurately, and this skill depends on maintaining a proper hold and a sharp knife.

The most popular knife for marquetry is the disposable blade, *hobby knife*. Bodies for hobby knives are available in a variety of sizes with an assortment of blades to fit. The blades for these knives are very sharp and quite thin. The acutely shaped blades will cut a very tight radius, but their flexibility can make them hard to control. They also tend to break when forced. That's why I shy away from the small acutely shaped blades and prefer the more obtuse.

*Photo 2*

Another handy knife to have in your assortment is the *utility knife*. The disposable blades for this knife are much stronger than the blades of the hobby knife, and the tool may be used for much heavier work.

*Photo 3*

My favorite knife is the *linoleum* or *floor covering knife*. This knife was designed for the kind of complex cutting found in marquetry. The cutting tip is as pointed as the most acute hobby knife, but the much thicker blade is not

*Photo 4*

so susceptible to flexing, which enhances control. And, the design of the knife permits a clear view of the line being cut. The linoleum knife will need to be sharpened periodically, and for this you will need a sharpening stone. I prefer the small ceramic stones shown in the photo 4.

Just because the blades for both hobby and utility knives are disposable doesn't mean you can't sharpen them. You can use a stone, either ceramic or hard Arkansas. Neither of these requires a "lubricant." Oilstones could be used, but they are messy and you will need an extremely fine stone to approach the sharpness of a factory-sharpened blade. I prefer to use a strop loaded with jewelers rouge, as shown in photo 5. A few passes over the strop can render a blade sharper than new.

*Photo 5*

No matter your choice of knife, there are some common cutting considerations:

*Don't try to cut the veneer in one pass.* Some veneers, (such as mahogany, walnut, hare wood and pine), can be cut in just one pass, but it generally takes at least two. And when it comes to zebra and ebony, it's time to get out your fret saw. A delicate knife, plus a tough, raw veneer equals one broken blade or worse—one inaccurate cut. Make several passes. Try to think of your knife as a saw with one tooth. To enhance cutting accuracy, make your first pass with a little more pressure than the weight of the knife itself. This establishes a path for your second pass and minimizes the tendency of the blade to follow the grain. With each subsequent pass, increase the pressure until the veneer is cut through. After the path of the cut has been established by the first couple passes, the blade will follow that path with little effort on your part. (Always cut *away from* rather than *toward* delicate areas that might split or chip away from the sheet by the forward pressure of your knife.)

*A knife is V-shaped.* As it cuts, it imparts this V-shape to the veneer, as shown in figure 6. The joint of two pieces of knife-cut veneer will be open or beveled at the top. This is not a big deal, because the V or bevel was formed by the knife · *compressing* the veneer; the knife didn't actually remove any material. Besides, when it comes time to bond your project, the moisture of the bonding adhesive will soak into the veneer—this will most likely relieve the compression and the joint will be tight.

**30**

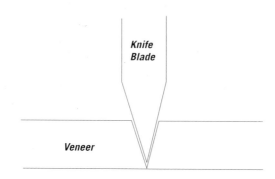

Figure 6

*Hold on.* For making straight cuts or curved cuts with gentle sweeps, choose an obtuse blade, or hold your acute blade at a low angle, as demonstrated in photo 6. The larger the portion of the blade in contact with the veneer, the easier it is to control. For tighter curves, raise the cutting angle as required (see photo 7). If you find a very tight

radius that can't be cut even with the knife held vertically, try stabbing cuts, as shown in photo 8. With this type of cut you slice forward and down instead of pulling the blade through the veneer. (Stabbing cuts can also be used to re-establish the path of a blade that has wandered.)

Photo 6

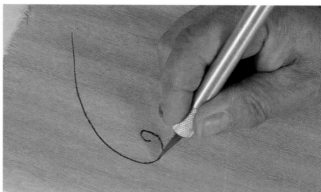

Photo 7

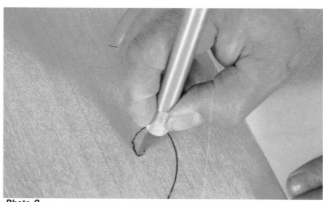

Photo 8

## SCISSORS

Use scissors to cut veneer? In a word, "yes." I'm not talking about that delicate pair of scissors in your sewing kit or desk drawer; I'm talking about a heavy-duty pair like those used by upholsterers or carpet layers—a pair with at least 8-inch (20 cm) blades. These are quite expensive, so if you don't want to make the investment, try a good pair of *tin snips* instead. No matter what you choose—scissors or snips—keep them sharp. If you tell the folks at the sharpening shop what you're cutting, they may adjust the cutting angle slightly, making them work even better. (The cutting angle of scissors should be slightly more obtuse, while the cutting angle of snips should be slightly more acute.)

## SAWS AND ACCESSORIES

There are two saws of particular interest to the marquetarian. The first of these is the *veneer saw.* See photo 9. It consists of a handle attached to a flat blade with a curved edge that has tiny saw teeth filed in it. Used in conjunction with a straightedge, a veneer saw is an excellent tool for making straight cuts.

(Never being satisfied with an off-the-shelf tool, I have modified my veneer saw by sharpening it like a knife and re-filing the teeth into a rip-saw configuration rather than the crosscut configuration of the off-the-shelf version. See figure 7. I find that my modified version cuts far more cleanly and may be either pushed or pulled. Since there is no set to the teeth, it doesn't grind away at the straightedge.)

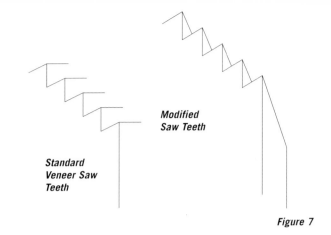

**Standard Veneer Saw Teeth**

**Modified Saw Teeth**

Figure 7

Photo 10

The second saw of interest is the *fret saw.* See photo 10, lower. This consists of a handle attached to a steel frame that stresses a tiny jeweler's saw blade. It has a 12-inch-deep (30.5 cm) throat, making it very useful for large projects. It accepts 5-inch (12.7 cm) blades and is designed especially for marquetry. At first, this saw is rather hard to control because of the 12-inch (30.5 cm) frame, but you will get used to it...probably after a few broken blades.

Another handy fret saw is actually a jeweler's saw. See photo 10, upper. It has a 2 ½-inch (6.4 cm) throat, which limits the size of the pieces you can cut. On the plus side, it is easier to control and will accept any length of blade, (which gives you something to do with all the blades you'll break with the regular fret saw). This is a great saw to use for small projects.

Blades for these saws range from #6/0 (very fine) to #5 (rather coarse). I use #3/0 and #4/0 for most cutting. I have #5 for cutting shapes in thin substrates. The finer blades cut very smoothly and

Photo 9

**CUTTING AND TAPING VENEER**

take a very small *kerf.* (The kerf refers to the void left from the material removed by the saw blade.) The #5, on the other hand, takes a much wider kerf and will destroy many delicate veneers. If you are a beginner, I recommend you practice with #1/0 blades before progressing to the #3/0 or #4/0.

You will need a couple of accessories for your fret saw. The first is a *bird's mouth.* This is a board with a "V" cut in the end, which is used to support the veneer, as shown in photo 11. My bird's mouth is ½ x 4 ½ x 30 inches (1.3 x 11.4 x 76.2 cm) and has a V-cut in both ends. On one end, the cut is 1 ⅛ inch (2.85 cm) wide at the mouth and tapers to 0 in 5 inches (12.7 cm). On the other end, the cut is 1¾ inch (4.4 cm) at the mouth and again tapers to 0 in 5 inches (12.7 cm).

Another required accessory is a small drill, like the one in photo 12, for boring holes in your veneer. This allows you to thread your blade and cut through the hole from the inside of the sheet, as shown in photo 13. Small hobby drills work well for this. See photo 14. I made my own by sticking a ⅟32-inch (.8 mm) bit in a wire nut filled with wet epoxy. See photo 15.

Once you've drilled a starter hole and passed the blade—clamped in the frame end—through, turn over the saw, compress the frame, and clamp the blade in the handle end, as shown in photo 16. (Make sure the teeth are pointed down.)

The cutting is done near the base or crotch of the V where the bird's mouth best supports the veneer. The first time you try using the fret saw, you may feel like the proverbial "one-armed paper hanger." It requires practice and perseverance to saw with one hand, move the veneer with the other, and actually make an accurate cut along your pattern line. Believe me, with a little practice, you'll become proficient. Try sitting directly behind the bird's mouth, the way I am in photo 17. Rest your elbow on your knee; this will give your wrist and forearm a reference in relation to the bird's mouth. See photo 18.

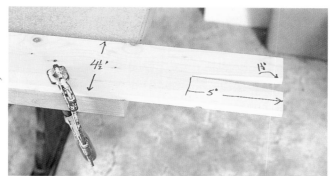

**Photo 11**

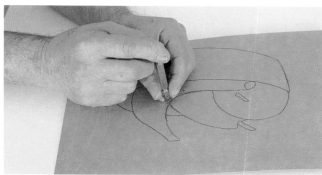

**Photo 12**

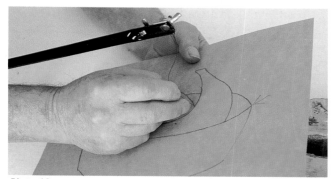

**Photo 13**

**Photo 14**

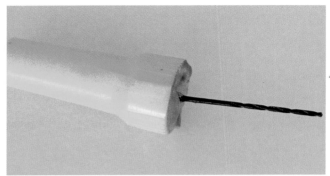
Photo 15

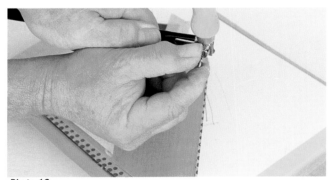
Photo 16

Photo 17

Photo 18

strokes will make the blade become dull in the center, and it will tend to bind as it is moved out of the dull area. On occasion, you may get an imperfect blade. If you find that a blade seems to bind in one area, replace it.

Several power jigsaws on the market accept jeweler's saw blades. I don't own one. I did. I bought it to cut some buffalo heads out of imitation ivory (sliced Tonga nuts) to inlay in some pool-table rails I was restoring. This was a moderately priced saw and well within my budget. After playing with it for about an hour, I found it did not work well for the imitation ivory and worked only slightly better on veneer. To boot, the vibration made my hand go numb. When I returned it to the store, the sales clerk directed me to a better saw, a fine piece of heavy-duty machinery. It handled the ivory and veneer gently and with great precision. It was also the most expensive jigsaw in the store and out of my budget. Moral? If you are going to buy a power saw, get a good one.

**33**

Keep the frame of the saw in line with the bird's mouth and turn the material being cut to accommodate the pattern. For an acute change of direction, keep the blade moving up and down as you rotate the veneer. This will prevent the blade from being twisted out of shape.

Do not force the blade forward in the veneer. Rather, concentrate on moving the saw up and down smoothly. It will advance all by itself. Use long strokes, the full length of the blade. Short

## WOOD-CARVING TOOLS

Quality carving tools are expensive, and I certainly wouldn't suggest that you run out and invest in a top-of-the-line set. Still, there are some economical sets available. Further, the manufacturers of hobby knives sell wood-carving gouges to fit their handles. I used one of these to cut ("punch" might be a better word) all of those musical notes on the CD cabinet door on page 82. It beat anything else I could think of.

## PAPER CUTTER

I can't leave this section on cutting without mentioning the paper cutter. If you have a straight-line geometrical project in mind, the paper cutter will be most handy. I call it a poor man's veneer shear. I was once commissioned to build a veneered conference table with a 4-inch-wide (10.2 cm) border consisting of more than 800 triangles of different species. I called an office-supply store and inquired about the price of a paper cutter—it was well within my budget. That afternoon, on my way to the office supply, I passed a thrift store and discovered a paper cutter there that cost next to nothing. Back at my shop, I taped a piece of paper to the table, carefully drew the outline of the triangles on it, and proceeded to make quick work of those 800-plus triangles. For repetitive angled cuts, a very useful trick is to place a couple of layers of masking tape on the cutter table to provide a stop. See photo 18.

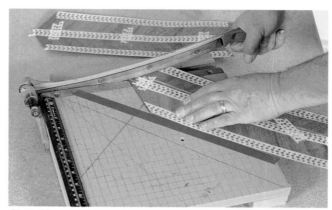

**Photo 18**

**34**

## ADJUSTING CUTS

Regardless of the cutting tool you use, you will make imperfect cuts. These imperfect cuts can create tiny gaps between the pieces of your project. (In the section on Bonding, we'll see how adhesives can help close up these gaps.) But, sometimes you can *adjust* imperfect cuts. If you have a cut that's a little long, the edge of the veneer can be whittled (with the grain) to the correct size, as shown in photo 19. If the direction of the grain or the shape of the piece make whittling impractical, use an ordinary emery board, as shown in photo 20. If you want to get fancy, glue some heavy-duty sandpaper to various shaped sticks. For those inside curves, wrap some sandpaper around a dowel or a pencil, as in photo 21.

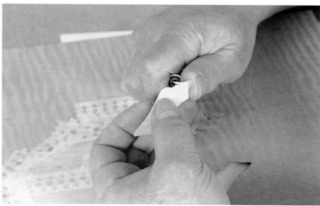

**Photo 19**

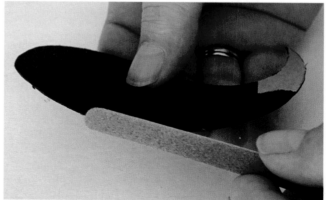

**Photo 20**

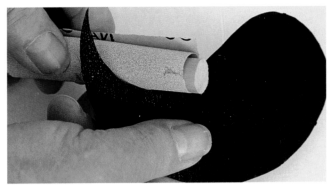
*Photo 21*

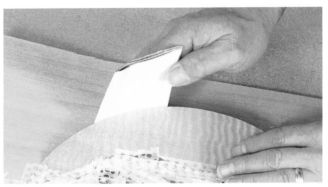
*Photo 22*

Sometimes just a piece of folded sandpaper will work. See photo 22.

If you have a cut that's a little short, you are not so fortunate. I once read a description of tightening a veneer joint after bonding with a little glue and a ball-peen hammer. I snickered. I snickered, that is, until I had a joint that didn't fit quite as well as it should have. Recalling the article, I forced a tiny bit of yellow glue into the open joint, and with the round end of the ball-peen hammer, I gently tapped the veneer about ¼ inch (6 mm) on either side of the joint. To my amazement, the hammer forced some fibers into the joint and the glue held them. I carefully scraped off the excess glue and walked away with a big grin.

At times, the best solution to an imperfect cut is to—you guessed it—cut out the piece again.

# CUTTING TECHNIQUES

There are several ways to accomplish the layout and cutting of a marquetry project. All are good. There is no *one* best. In the following, I'll present a number of techniques for your consideration. Adapt these to your own needs. I strongly advise that you not limit yourself to one technique. If you do, you will find yourself working with one hand tied. You see, each has merit and there is no law that says you can't use all of them in a single project.

## PATTERN CUTTING

*Pattern cutting* is very simple. You need a full-scale pattern and a selection of veneers, as shown in photo 23. First, cut out all the individual pieces of your full-scale drawing. See photo 24. Then, place the individual pattern pieces on the appropriate veneers and trace the shapes onto the

*Photo 23*

*Photo 24*

**Photo 25**

veneers, as shown in photo 25. You can trace the pattern pieces with a pencil first, or start right out with your knife.

Here are a few things to keep in mind when using this method:

First, draw your pattern on heavy paper. Use old file folders, card stock from the office-supply store, poster board, or bakery boxes. Just make sure you use something more substantial than typing paper.

**36**

Second, don't use your fingers to hold the pattern piece onto the veneer. The piece will probably slip, and it's very tricky to get it back into the exact position. Also, you could cut yourself...I've got the scars to prove it. Instead, use metal push pins to keep your pattern pieces secure. You may tap these into place with a hammer, if necessary. For delicate veneers, where the pinholes will present a challenge, or with veneers you wish to cut with scissors or some other unorthodox tool—use rubber cement. It will hold the pattern securely, and the residue can be easily cleaned from the veneer with a brisk rubbing. (See page 53 for working with rubber cement.)

Once each piece is cut, adjust your cuts, if necessary, as described above. Now you're ready to proceed to taping up your project.

## WINDOW CUTTING

*Window cutting* is the most frequently used method of cutting and fitting a marquetry project. First, the pattern is transferred to the background veneer or a temporary background veneer called a *waster*. Use tracing and carbon paper, or transfer paper, or the laser copy heat transfer technique described on page 25, to transfer your pattern onto the veneer. Hinge your pattern to the background veneer with tape to maintain correct register.

Now you are ready to cut a project piece out of the background veneer, creating a hole or *window* through which you can try out your different contrasting veneers until you find the one that looks best. First, tape the contrasting veneer you've chosen to the back of the background veneer to prevent it from slipping, as shown in photo 26. You also can use metal push pins to secure it. Now, use the window as a template and mark the chosen veneer with a very sharp pencil. (A .5mm mechani-

**Photo 26**

cal pencil works well, as shown in photo 27, but let the lead, rather than the sleeve, ride against the edge of the window.) You can use the tip of a knife to mark with, but cut very lightly. See photo 28. Then, remove the piece and continue cutting. The knife tip *mark* will establish a path for the cut, making the process much easier. This works well except where marks are made with the grain. These tend to get lost, so mark these with a pencil. Once the contrasting piece has been cut out, tape it into the window with perforated veneer tape.

I usually start by marking and cutting the largest window first. It's not necessary to fit the total periphery of some pieces to the background. You'll notice in photo 29 that I'm using a straightedge to cut the area above the mark for the top of the bowl. Windows will be cut in that area for other pieces, as shown in photo 30, so there is no need to fit the bowl perfectly there. Continue to cut windows in the background and replace them with your choice of contrasting veneers, until you have completed the picture. Most of the background will be replaced in this manner.

Unless you are far better at window cutting than I am, the pieces will not always fit perfectly into the window. They may, of course be trimmed as described in Adjusting Cuts on page 34. Sometimes a little pressure exerted with the back of a knife will force them into place, as shown in photo 31. Another little trick for getting those slightly oversize pieces to fit is to run the tip of a knife along the joint (see photo 32). The object is not to *cut*, but to use the knife as a wedge to *compress* the veneers and force the piece into place.

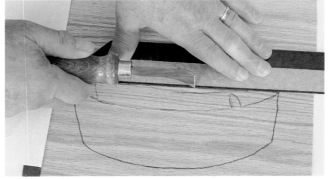
**Photo 29**

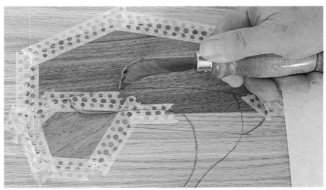
**Photo 30**

**37**

**Photo 27**

**Photo 31**

**Photo 28**

**Photo 32**

## INLAY

I guess you could call *inlay* "reverse window cutting," because that's exactly what is. First, a project piece is cut out. Then, this piece is used as a template to mark the background veneer. The background veneer is then cut, and the project piece is inserted. I often use this technique when I have to cut a difficult shape in a hard-to-cut species. Once the piece is cut, I can inlay it into the easier-to-cut background. Sometimes the design centers on one particular piece, such as the Gift Wrapped Box project on page 102. Here, the bow and ribbon were cut first, then the background was marked and cut to fit the pieces. See photo 33. The bow and pieces of ribbon were inlayed into the background. A small carving tool is used to fit the ribbon to the bow, as shown in photo 34.

*Photo 33*

*Photo 34*

## SPECIAL INLAY TECHNIQUES

When your pattern requires very thin strips of veneer—for the whiskers of a cat, wires strung between power poles, or the fine lines of a typeface—wait until *after* you've bonded your project to inlay them.

First, holding the knife perpendicular to the surface, make a cut slightly to one side of the desired inlayed strip. See photo 35. Next, turn the project around and reposition the straightedge just slightly. Make a diagonal cut that will meet the first at the backside of the veneer, as shown in photo 36. (If you're cutting cross-grain, the veneer should chip away easily. If you're working with the grain, you will have to make a stabbing cut at each end of the parallel cuts in order to free the piece.)

To cut a strip to be inlayed, trim the edge of a piece of contrasting veneer. Then move your straightedge slightly and cut off a thin strip at a 45° angle, as shown in photo 37. You'll note that I'm partial to a veneer saw for this operation. (The exact angle of these cuts can be adjusted to accommodate different widths of strips. Before attempting this operation on your project, practice on some scraps.) Trim the strip to the desired length.

Spread a tiny bead of glue in the bottom of the V-shaped groove you made in the background and install the strip. Gluing is likely to be messy, so I use hide glue. Then, I cover the glued strips with weights, or I clamp a block of wood over the assembly. A sheet of waxed paper will keep the glue from sticking to the wood block. Once dry, the hide glue is quite easy to sand off.

**Photo 35**

**Photo 36**

**Photo 37**

## PAD CUTTING

Another method is called *pad cutting*. Here, full-size pieces of all the different types of veneer used in a project are stacked and taped together around the edges—or held with rubber cement—to form a pad. See photo 38. The pattern is transferred to the top veneer, and a fret saw is used to cut out all the pieces. It's important that all the grains run in the desired direction for the particular pieces.

This method can be somewhat wasteful. In the Christmas Tree Ornaments project on page 107, I used all of the pieces I cut. With the fruit bowl I'm making to demonstrate the technique, only *one* set of components will be the proper colors. However, there are some roads to economy. You can tape a precious piece of veneer into a window cut in a cheaper species. In photo 39, I taped a piece of satin wood, which I'll use for the pear, into a piece of the poster board I used as a cutting surface. I also taped a piece of burl, which I'll use for the two small interior bowl pieces, to the pad. See photo 40. These components will be cut first, and the burl waste stripped from the pad. It is important that the pad be flat, giving support to all of the veneers.

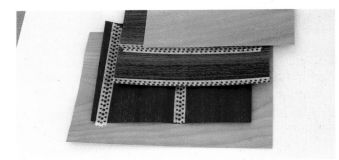

**Photo 38**

**39**

**Photo 39**

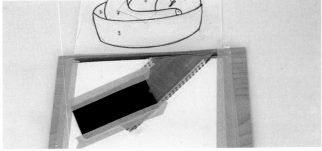

**Photo 40**

I usually transfer a mirror image of the pattern to the underside of the background, since it is somewhat larger than the component pieces that are taped to it. Before you start cutting, sweep the floor. Some of your smaller pieces usually wind up there, and you don't want to confuse them with any scraps or trimmings. Then, begin cutting, starting with the smallest components first. It is very important that the saw blade is kept perpendicular to the pad. Otherwise, the components will not fit properly. As the cutting progresses, the pad can become quite flimsy, so reinforce the holes with masking tape. See photo 41. Once the sawing is complete, separate the layers using a sharp knife, or for larger pieces, a putty knife. Then, it's just a matter of assembling the jigsaw puzzle. At first, just *tack* the components in with *tiny* pieces of tape, as shown in photo 42. Lots of wet tape can cause swelling, making positioning and assembling difficult.

Gentle Reader, I have a confession. I could not force myself to toss all of the leftover pieces in the trash. I assembled another set. If someone questions the color scheme, I, with a straight face, will say, "Oh that's the negative. That's what the picture looked like before it was developed." Then, I went ahead and assembled two more sets. Maybe I can convince someone that these are printer's color separations. If they buy that, I'll see if I can sell them my gold mine stock.

**40**

Photo 42

# BEVEL CUTTING

A variation of pad cutting called *bevel cutting* eliminates the gap left by the saw blade. To bevel cut, the piece to be cut is taped—or held with rubber cement—to the underside of the background veneer. The piece is cut out with the fret saw held at about a 10° angle. When the cut piece is inserted into the front of the background veneer, the angle of the pieces takes up the gap of the blade. See figure 8.

Isn't that clever? Clever it is, but there are a couple of things I should mention. If you are using a power saw, it's easy to tilt the table. If you are using a fret saw, tilt the bird's mouth and keep the saw working in a vertical manner. To tilt the bird's mouth, I place a couple of wedges beneath it before clamping it to my bench, as shown in photo 43.

If you will be using a water-based adhesive for bonding bevel-cut pieces, tape each in place securely. It's even a good idea to spread a tiny bit of glue in the joint. Use all of the pressing force you can. When the moisture from the water-based adhesive gets to the veneers, both will swell, and the joint could slide apart leaving a hump in the veneers and a void in the glue line, as shown in figure 9.

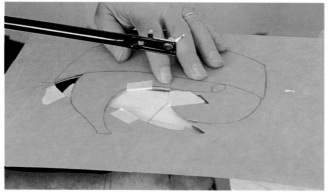

Photo 41

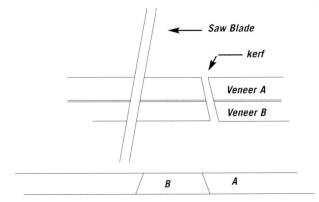

Saw Blade

kerf

Veneer A

Veneer B

B    A

*Figure 8*

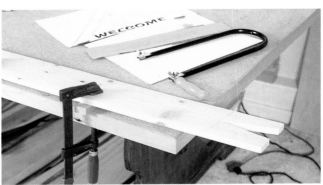

*Photo 43*

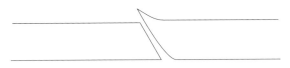

*Figure 9*

## TAPING VENEERS

To hold all of the pieces of a marquetry project together prior to bonding, you tape it. The best tape for the job is gummed-paper veneer tape. There are two types readily available. The first is 1-inch-wide (2.5 cm) heavy paper tape. See photo 44. It is the stronger of the two and should always be used when strength is required. This tape is always applied to the face of the project. (If it is applied to the back, it prevents the bonding glue from reaching the veneer.) The other type of veneer tape is perforated and much thinner than the solid tape. See photo 45. You'll note in the photos throughout this book that the thin tape is usually my tape of choice. The perforated tape has the advantage of letting you see the joints you are taping. In addition, it may be applied in small quantities to the back of a project, because the glue can still reach the veneer through the perforations.

*Photo 44*

*Photo 45*

To moisten the tape, I use a sponge stuffed in a cup filled with water to about 1 inch (2.5 cm) below the surface of the sponge. See photo 46. Don't lick the tape. I don't know of any mint-flavored tape, and you don't want marquetry to "leave a bad taste in your mouth."

Once you've moistened the gummed side of the tape, move it quickly to the joint and press it down with your fingers, as shown in photo 47. You may have to hold or rub it for a few seconds until the adhesive grabs. The tape should dry for a few minutes before the joint is handled. If you require maximum strength immediately, warm the tape with an iron set at *silk*.

Often you will have a lot of tape on a project, over-lapping in several areas. As this tape dries, it can pull the face of the project—cupping it or wrinkling it. To remedy this, moisten the untaped side of the project with a damp cloth, or mist it very lightly with a spray bottle. Then, iron it flat with the iron at the *wool* setting. Iron until the project is dry.

Many layers of overlapping tape—especially the heavier tape—can pose challenges when it comes time to bond using a press. Try to use no more than three layers of heavy tape or five layers of the lighter.

Once a project is bonded, remove the tape. Some marquetarians suggest sanding it off. I don't. Sanding leaves paper residue in the pores of open-grain woods and can actually result in an uneven surface. I prefer to rewet the tape, using a small brush. Rewet only the tape; don't saturate the surrounding veneer. See photo 48. After the water has soaked in for a minute or two, the tape can be peeled off. If you're in a hurry, use a scraper. Even an ordinary spatula will work, as shown in photo 49.

*Photo 46*

*Photo 47*

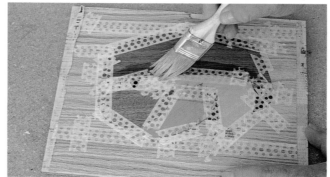

*Photo 48*

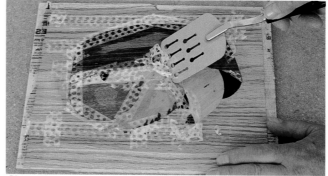

*Photo 49*

# GROUNDS

Marquetry projects must be bonded (or glued) to something for support. This "something" is referred to as the *substrate* or more commonly, the *ground*. Most grounds are made from wood or wood-fiber products, but with an adequate adhesive, your project may be bonded to any clean, smooth surface, and that surface need not be flat.

## CONDITIONS

Before choosing a ground for bonding your marquetry project, you should be aware of some particular conditions. These conditions occur due to the interactions of the ground material, the bonding adhesive, and the veneers. An understanding of these conditions will help you avoid unnecessary work and ensure project satisfaction.

## STABILITY

The ground you choose to bond your project to must be stable. Undue dimensional changes in the ground material can ruin a lot of hard work by causing your project to check or crack. Extreme dimensional changes can also cause your bond to fail. To create maximum stability, allow both the veneers and the ground to acclimate to your environmental conditions for several days before bonding. Applying marquetry to a metal ground that will be exposed to temperature extremes is not recommended, nor should you ever bond a project to uncured lumber.

## PULL

When using a water-based adhesive to bond wood veneer, the ground will be subjected to a condition called *pull*. The veneer can pull on the ground material causing it to cup. Why? Well, as the moisture of the glue disperses through the veneer and ground, both expand, but the veneer expands far more than the ground. Usually a strong bond develops before all of the residual moisture leaves. As this moisture does leave, the veneer shrinks more than the ground.

Pull may range from barely noticeable to dramatic, depending on the tenacity of the ground material and the type of veneer. The Welcome Sign project on page 98 pulled the ¼-inch (6 mm) faced MDF ground material less than ⅛-inch (3 mm). Had I bonded it to a ¾-inch (1.9 cm) MDF ground, the pull would have probably gone unnoticed.

Here's a worst case scenario: If you were to bond a large wall hanging, say 2 x 3 feet (60 x 90 cm), and you immediately framed it, pull could destroy the frame and even break the glass.

The obvious solution to pull is to use an adhesive other than the water-based types. There's good news and bad news here, and we'll talk more on the subject in the next section. (Also, I'll present a method of bonding using an inexpensive, safe, water-based adhesive with little or no danger of pull. I'll also share a trick on press bonding that minimizes pull.)

Another solution is to balance things out by veneering the *backside* of the ground with a similar, but less costly veneer. Even bits and pieces can be used on the back. In photo 1 I bonded less costly pieces that I didn't even take the time to join well. In most cases this solution works very well. In some projects, especially those in which a variety of veneers are used, or where the grains

*Photo 1*

run in all directions—veneering both sides of the ground may not be the complete solution.

Should you complete a project and find some intolerable cupping of the ground, all is not lost. Wait until the glue is thoroughly cured, and the moisture of the glue has completely evaporated. This will take several days. Then, heat the project to about 150°F (65°C). If the project is small, this may be done in an oven. (Put a pan of water in the bottom of the oven to keep the project from getting too dry.) If the project is too large for the oven, it may be heated by wrapping it in black plastic film or a dark plastic trash bag and placing it in the sun on a summer day. After the project is heated through, clamp it to some heavy material, bending it slightly in the opposite direction of the cup. See photo 2. When the project has completely cooled, it will be flat or at least flatter—several treatments may be necessary to completely flatten it.

# TELEGRAPHING

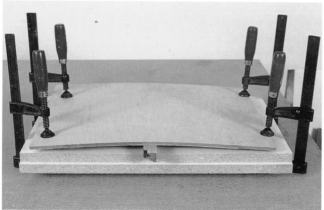

Photo 2

Another condition to be aware of is called *telegraphing*. Irregularities in the surface of the ground may telegraph, or find their way, to the surface of the project. Dings, mars, and a rough ground surface will fill with excess glue. When that glue dries and shrinks, it will pull down the veneer in an irregular manner. See figure 10. In many projects, telegraphing is completely inconspicuous, but in a highly polished tabletop, these defects will be less than attractive.

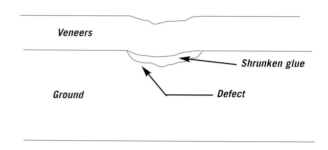

Figure 10

Another kind of telegraphing can occur when an edge banding is applied to a ground; both the ground and the edge banding swell slightly at the glue line. If the glue line is sanded before the glue has thoroughly dried, the swelling will be cut level with the surface. If the project is then bonded, shrinkage will pull the veneers into a small valley at the glue line. See figure 11.

To deal with defects that have telegraphed to the surface, let the project dry for a week or so. It's imperative that the glue is dry and no moisture is left in the ground or veneers before you sand the surface level and smooth.

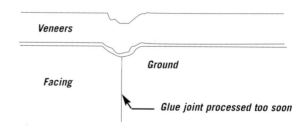

Figure 11

# GROUND MATERIALS

## MEDIUM DENSITY FIBERBOARD (MDF)

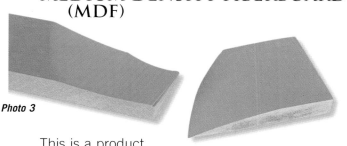

**Photo 3**

This is a product composed of wood that has been reduced to its fiber state, mixed with an adhesive, and pressed into a board. This is an excellent marquetry ground. MDF is available in thicknesses of ¼ inch to 1½ inches (6 mm to 3.8 cm). It is very stable and quite tenacious, and you can bond a small project to the thicker varieties with little or no noticeable pull.

MDF has a glazed surface, so scuff it with coarse sandpaper before bonding. It is also quite heavy. If weight is a concern, consider the materials mentioned below.

## HARDBOARD

This is another product composed of wood reduced to its fiber state, and it's a fine marquetry ground, especially when a thin stable ground is required. It is very similar to MDF, but only readily available in ⅛ inch (3 mm) and ¼ inch (6 mm) thicknesses. Hardboard is best suited to marquetry pictures that are to be framed, and it should be veneered on both sides.

When selecting hardboard, choose the *tempered* variety. It is slightly heavier, but more tenacious and less susceptible to cupping. It is also glazed, which can prevent a good bond, so you'll need to break that glaze by sanding with coarse (80-grit) sandpaper.

Better yet, choose the *faced* variety, shown in photo 4. It is called MDF, but it's actually veneered hardboard. You'll probably find the birch- or

**Photo 4**

maple-faced variety less expensive. For all of the thin projects I did for this book, I used ¼-inch (6 mm) birch-faced hardboard as a ground material. This faced veneer does not require scuffing and always seems to bond easily to the project. It's relatively expensive, but worth the extra cost.

## PARTICLEBOARD

This material is composed of particles of wood that are about the consistency of coarse sawdust. Particleboard is quite heavy, but it's a perfectly acceptable ground for a marquetry project and is available in a

**Photo 5**

variety of thicknesses. Even though this ground is stable, if you use a water-based adhesive, you should still veneer both sides to avoid pull. When purchasing particleboard, choose the type intended for cabinets, rather than the flooring and sheathing type.

## PLYWOOD

Plywood is made by laminating an odd number of veneers together. The grain of each veneer runs perpendicular to the grain of the veneer next to it. This is a strong, stable, versatile board. It's available in thicknesses ranging from ⅛ inch to 1⅛ inches (3 mm to 3.25 cm).

**Photo 6**

45

Plywood is much lighter than the fiber products mentioned above.

Plywood makes an excellent ground material, but all plywood is not created equal. Avoid fir plywood. Although it may look and feel smooth, it doesn't always stay that way. The best plywood for marquetry is marine-grade plywood. It's called Baltic Birch or Apple Maple where I shop. It is composed of hardwood veneers throughout—usually birch or maple. Marine plywood is bonded with waterproof glue and is very stable. It is also more expensive, but the investment is well worth it.

## PARTICLEBOARD-FACED VENEER CORE PLYWOOD

This is a wonderful combination of fiber products and plywood. This material has a plywood core with a thin layer of particleboard bonded to each side. A hardwood face veneer is bonded over the particleboard—birch or maple is the most economical.

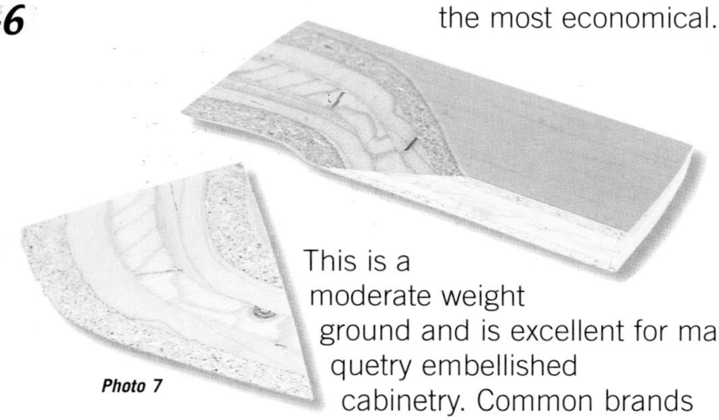

*Photo 7*

This is a moderate weight ground and is excellent for marquetry embellished cabinetry. Common brands are Pro-core, Classy Core, and Gold Core.

## FLAKE BOARD

Like fir plywood, flake board—also called waffle board or chip board—is another product intended for the construction industry. It consists of many

*Photo 8*

flakes of softwood veneer pressed together to make a building board, which is fine for floors and sheathing. As a marquetry ground, it's less than perfect. If you do use flake board, bond your project to the side that looks like a waffle iron. If you're using a water-based adhesive, make sure you veneer the other side to counter pull.

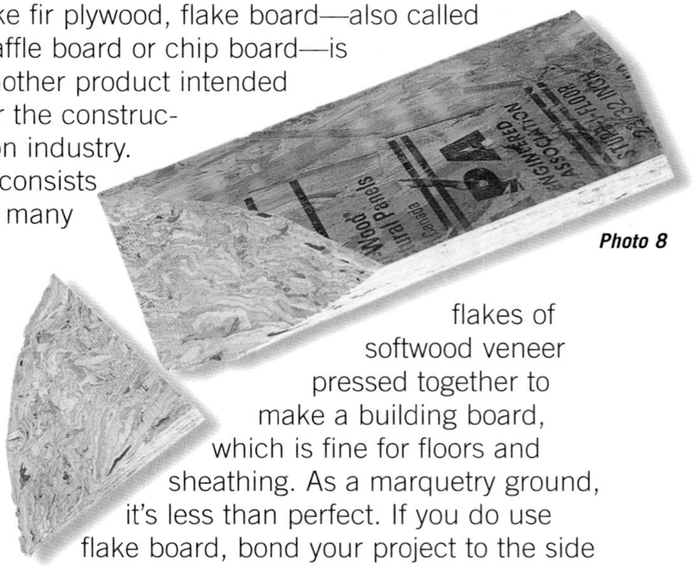

## SOLID WOOD

With all the other materials available, I can't imagine using solid wood as a marquetry ground, unless it happened to be a cabinet you wanted to embellish with artwork. Solid wood is most susceptible to pull. Defects, such as knots, will telegraph, especially if the wood isn't thoroughly cured. Glue joints will telegraph unless they are allowed to dry completely before the panel is processed. Should you find yourself applying a project to solid wood—perhaps a raised door panel or an old tabletop—be sure the wood is well cured. In the case of an old tabletop, whose finish has been removed with paint remover, allow several days for the water wash to dry. Fill any defects with nitrocellulose putty or auto-body putty, and make sure the underside is veneered and well sealed.

46

# EDGE TREATMENTS FOR MANUFACTURED BOARDS

The edges of MDF, particleboard, and especially plywood, are not pretty. If your project is to be framed, this won't be an issue because the edges will be hidden. But if your project is a tabletop or a cabinet, you certainly don't want to be looking at the raw edges of a piece of plywood.

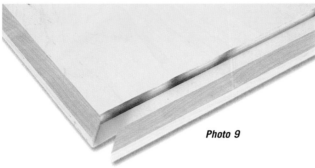

*Photo 9*

You can veneer the edges of any of the manufactured boards we've discussed. If you want a molded edge, simply glue a strip of solid wood that is wide enough to receive the mold, plus about ¼ inch (6 mm) to the edge. See photo 9. The strip of solid wood should be slightly thicker than the board, so it can be scraped or sanded flush with the surface. Wait several days before sanding or scraping, so the glue line won't telegraph to the surface.

# NONWOOD GROUND MATERIALS

Marquetry may be applied to a variety of surfaces. Here are a couple of alternative grounds to consider.

# METAL

Marquetarians need not limit themselves to wood; metals make a fine ground. The canisters on page 89 are lightweight steel. I once decorated a metal file cabinet with some very fine veneers. While I was not very enthusiastic about the commission at the onset, my indifference turned to excitement as the work progressed. After rolling the cabinet out of the paint shop, I had a real sense of pride at what I initially thought would be an abomination.

A couple of things to think about when applying wood veneer over metal: wood changes dimensionally with changes in its moisture content, while metal does not. Any wood veneer applied over metal should be completely dry. Also, the veneer should have a good finish applied to it after bonding to protect it from seasonal humidity changes. Otherwise, the veneer could pull the metal, especially unsupported metal, like the sides of the file cabinet I mentioned.

# GLASS

Why would anyone want to apply marquetry over glass? Sound like a good question? Well not to me. Imagine a very plain mirror framed in marquetry applied directly to the glass. Imagine a windowpane with a tiny vine and flowers embroidered in it marquetry-style. Are you beginning to get ideas? Hope so...the opportunity is there.

**47**

# GLUES

Technically, glue is not an adhesive. Nevertheless, I'll use the words *glue* and *adhesive* interchangeably as have so many of my colleagues who have gone this way before.

Glue, Gentle Reader, is what we use to bond our marquetry to our ground. Our choice of ground material will often determine the proper glue for the job, since all adhesives are not created equal. A variety of adhesives can be used for marquetry. The glues I'll describe are reasonably priced, readily available, and will serve the needs of the marquetarian well.

Some of the glues used in marquetry are quite safe to use; others are not so safe. To judge the risks involved with using the not-so-safe glues, I did a quick inventory and some safety research on other products that might be found in the home. The cautions on drain cleaners, toilet-bowl cleaners, and some laundry products, are downright scary; so are the cautions on oven cleaners and some silver cleaners and polishes. Some aerosol and spray products contain cautions, but most omit the fact that inhaling the mist of these products can be very hazardous.

After my little bit of research, I feel that I'm far safer out in the workshop than in my own home.

## WATER-BASED GLUES

Water-based glues are the most readily available, and for the most part, the safest to use. As mentioned in the chapter on grounds, they cause a condition called *pull*. That little shortcoming aside, marquetarians probably find themselves using water-based glues ten-to-two.

## HOT HIDE GLUE

The mainstay of the woodworking industry from the time of the Pharaohs until WWII, hot hide glue is a safe, nontoxic adhesive made by rendering animal hides, bones, and hooves. Hot hide glue is available in dried flakes or granules, as shown in photo 1, both of which are soaked in water to soften. After they soften, they turn into jelly-like globs. The water is then poured off, and the substance is heated to about 150°F (65°C). The heat creates the very thick, sticky liquid you see in photo 2.

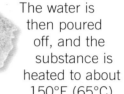

**Photo 1**

**Photo 2**

The hot glue is applied to the ground, and the veneer is set in place while the glue is still hot. As the glue cools to about 90°F (32°C), it congeals. It will hold somewhat at this point. After drying—usually overnight—the bond is complete.

There are equipment costs involved with the use of hot hide glue. The electric glue pot used for heating is the biggest expense. But you can heat the glue in a double-boiler arrangement on a range or hot plate to save some money. The ultimate set up is to place the double boiler on the

48

*Photo 3*

heating element of a coffee maker, as shown in photo 3. Most coffee makers are set to maintain a temperature of about 150°F (65°C). Check yours with a candy thermometer.

When I bond a project one piece at a time or do inlay work with fine lines (like the notes on the CD cabinet on page 82), I use hot hide glue. It's great for this kind of work. The initial adhesion, as the glue congeals, holds very well. If, for some reason, a piece has to be removed or adjusted, heating the piece with an iron will release it. Even after the glue has dried for several days, its action may be reversed. Simply wet the piece you want to remove and let the water soak in for a few minutes. Warm the area with an iron, and the glue will release.

I can be a bit untidy with glue, but this isn't a problem with hide glue. Hide glue won't seal veneer, and it can be easily sanded off once it's dry. The glue will fill open pores, but it's easily removed with a toothbrush once it congeals. Hide glue washes out of clothing easily, but hands are another story. I use warm water to immediately wash off any glue that gets on my hands. You see, hide glue is very sticky, and more than once I've found myself overly attached to pieces of veneer and assorted tools.

## LIQUID HIDE GLUE

If salt or urea is added to hot hide glue, it will lower the temperature at which it congeals. If enough is added, it will remain liquid at room temperature. Basically, *liquid* hide glue has the same characteristics as *hot* hide glue. Although it does not congeal, it's reversible with warm water and is safe to use. The main attraction to this glue is that it's slow to set or has a long *open time*. Consider using liquid hide glue if your pressing arrangement is slow and difficult to load.

## POLY VINYL ACETATE GLUES (PVA)

These water-based glues are extremely popular with hobbyists and general crafters. They are easy to use, and readily available.

**49**

*Photo 4*

## WHITE GLUE

Sometimes referred to as *white vinyl glue*, (photo 4) this product reigned as the workhorse of the woodworking industry from the end of WWII into the '70s, when its cousin *aliphatic resin glue* (yellow glue) came into general use. It is relatively safe to use, cleans up with water, and has a rather short set time—about 30 minutes. Clothing and hands wash up fine with warm water and soap.

On the minus side, white glue seals wood, so finishing products will not penetrate. Spots sealed with glue will appear as milky blotches under clear finishes. Though white glue may be sanded from the surface, it quickly clogs sandpaper. It turns clear as it dries, which makes it hard to see, so clean up the surface as soon as possible. (Sometimes I put a few drops of food coloring in my white glue to make it easier to see.)

Unlike the hide glues, white glue is *not* reversible. Soaking the glue joint with water will release it, but the process is slow, and fresh glue will have to be added to make a new bond. (White glue does have some fine thermoplastic properties, which we'll discuss on page 58.)

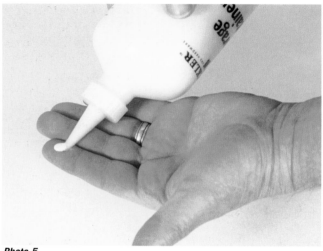
*Photo 5*

## YELLOW GLUE

*Yellow glue* is a higher grade of white glue and is used extensively in the woodworking industry today (photo 5). There are many specialty formulations of yellow glue available and all will work well for the marquetarian. Yellow glue has the same basic properties as white glue, but it has a stronger bond and a faster set time—about 20 minutes.

## WATER-RESISTANT YELLOW GLUE

This special formula is particularly suitable for outdoor or high humidity applications. Note the words "water resistant." This does not mean *waterproof.* Joints made with water-resistant yellow glue will release if soaked for long periods of time.

## UREA-FORMALDEHYDE

If your project calls for a glue that is highly resistant to water, consider *urea-formaldehyde.* Although it is toxic, its bond and water resistance are the greatest of any readily available, water-based adhesive. Be aware that after the glue begins to cure, spills cannot be removed from clothing in the wash, and any glue that gets on your skin will be difficult to remove. (You'll have to soak your hands in warm soapy water for quite a while. This could score some points from your mate if it's not your turn to do the dishes.)

Urea-formaldehyde is available as a liquid with a catalyst that's added just prior to use. See photo 6, left. This glue works through chemical action rather than the evaporation of the water base. It is also available as a powder (shown on the right in photo 6). In this form the catalyst is in the powder and is activated when water is added. Once mixed, the glue has a limited life. The container will give you specific instructions.

*Photo 6*

This glue is very *slow* to set and cure. At a working temperature of 70°F (21°C), glue joints should be clamped for 14 hours. Raising the working temperature will shorten this time dramatically. Heating your project with an iron can reduce the curing time to under an hour. For larger projects, you can preheat the ground and press components in an oven or with an electric blanket.

The formaldehyde component of this glue is toxic, so be sure to read and understand all of the cautions on the label.

# NONWATER-BASED GLUES

I mentioned a condition called pull (see page 42). The swelling of the veneer in contact with water-based adhesives causes this condition. If this condition intimidates you, or you have a project where pull cannot be overcome in any way, the following adhesives are for you.

*Photo 7*

## CONTACT CEMENT

*Contact cement* is quick, easy to use, and produces a satisfactory bond for most marquetry projects. For the metal kitchen canisters on page 87, it was the only practical glue (photo 7).

All contact cements are not created equal; there are water-based contact cements and exotic, non-flammable solvent-based contact cements. However, the only one I recommend is the flammable type. There are health hazards involved with all contact cements, but if you think the risks are high with the flammable variety, read the cautions on some of the nonflammable types. In addition, some of the nonflammable types have a strong, bad smell.

This product is quite flammable and fumes may ignite with explosive force, so read and understand all of the cautions printed on the container of contact cement. Although the amounts of contact cement used by the marquetarian will likely be small and pose a minimum explosion hazard, I'm going to mention something the containers often omit. The fumes are heavy. As you work with contact cement, your nose may tell you that there is no appreciable concentration of fumes in the work area. If your feet could talk, however they would tell a different story; since the fumes are heavy, the concentration will be near the floor. If you happen to be working in a basement with a gas water heater, extinguish the pilot light before spreading contact cement. Sources of ignition 30 inches (76 cm) or more above the floor and a good distance—20 feet (66 m)—from the work area pose less of a risk.

The joints of your project should fit quite snugly if you choose to use contact cement for bonding. Contact cement will *not* swell the joints closed like the water-based products will, and any contact that does fill a joint will interfere with your finishing mediums. It's no fun to clean contact cement from the surface of a project, so it's an excellent idea to tape all the joints to prevent the cement from getting there.

Contact cement is not easily removed from clothing. It can be removed from the project and the skin with solvents. Lacquer thinner will dissolve contact cement; but it also will drive it deeper into the wood and seal it. Lacquer thinner is also hard on the skin. Instead of lacquer thinner, use a solvent such as mineral spirits (paint thinner). With a little vigorous rubbing, mineral spirits will cause contact cement to ball up, and it's gentler on your skin. You can also use ordinary hand lotion or salad oil for hand cleaning. (NOTE: Paint thinner and lacquer thinner are also flammable liquids.)

Finishing products that contain lacquer thinner, such as dye stains and lacquer top coats, can cause contact cement to release. If your veneers were very flat and bonded easily, this shouldn't be a problem, but if your veneers were somewhat wrinkled and had to be forced down, the solvents in the finish could cause the contact cement bond to fail. Heat and pressure can also cause contact to release. Sunlight on dark veneers can warm them substantially. A warm serving platter or a steaming mug set on a tabletop could cause release.

Photo 8

# CYANOACRYLATE (CA)

This product is essentially uncured vinyl. (Photo 8.) There are different brands of this product available and it comes in three different viscosities. It is rather expensive, but I've found it great for bonding that little piece I just had to add after the project was complete. It's clear, colorless, and wonderful for bonding veneer to glass where the work will be viewed from both sides.

CA is safe and hazardous at the same time. It's not toxic. As a matter of fact, it's used in the emergency room as a substitute for stitches. I've tried it on cuts and it works. I've also used it to repair torn fingernails—works great. However, CA will bond to just about anything, so it can be hazardous. If you're going to use CA, make sure you also have a CA release agent (seen on the far right, in photo 8). It has become my practice, before opening any container of CA, to open the bottle of release agent and set it nearby. You see, Gentle Reader, I'm naturally sloppy and more than once I've found myself stuck to a project or tool. It's embarrassing to wander around the shop, stuck to something, asking if anyone has seen the release agent.

Keep CA off the face of your project. It will seal the wood and have to be sanded off. It clogs sandpaper, and the penetration of CA can be quite deep. This can result in blotches, even if only clear coats are used.

CA manufactures also supply an activator (shown second from right, in photo 8). You apply the CA to one surface to be bonded and the activator to the other. When the two come together the bond is immediate. CA is activated by moisture, and I've found that applying CA to one surface and exhaling on the other greatly speeds the bonding action.

I mentioned that CA is supplied in three viscosities; the two more viscous have some gap-filling properties and are recommended for wood. However, the bond is not as immediate—even with the activator—or as strong as the bond created with the least viscous type. I've obtained the most immediate and strongest bond by first priming—applying a thin coat to each surface—with the least viscous, then letting it dry for about 15 minutes, then applying the least viscous again.

Note: Safety glasses and latex gloves are in order when using CA.

**Photo 9**

## RUBBER CEMENT

Though worthless as a bonding agent, rubber cement has a place in marquetry. (Photo 9.) There may come a time when you want to pad-cut some veneers, and there is just no convenient way to tape or pin them together. Enter rubber cement— stage right. When used as directed, this product will hold the veneers together well enough for the pad-cut. After the cut is complete, the two pieces may be carefully separated. Remove the residues by rubbing briskly with your fingers. Use a toothbrush to remove residue from the pores of open-grain wood.

Continued and prolonged exposure to the fumes of rubber cement is not healthy, so work in a well-ventilated area and don't smoke. Rubber cement is very flammable. (Even if the resultant fire doesn't cause any serious damage, the thick, black, sticky smoke given off will have to be cleaned from everything in sight—been there, done that.)

## SPREADING GLUES BEFORE PRESSING

In pressing operations, you could dribble glue onto the ground and spread it around with a stick or your finger. You might get lucky and get a good even spread. More than likely you will have thick spots that waste glue and thin spots that won't bond. So, let's choose something a little more reliable.

## TOOTHED TROWEL

White and yellow glue (full-strength) and urea-formaldehyde are best spread with a *toothed trowel*. I've even used a trowel for contact cement (on plastic laminate, but never on veneers). These are available at your friendly, neighborhood home improvement center or lumberyard. The plastic, disposable ones are quite economical. Choose one with V-shaped teeth, spaced $3/32$ inches (2.3mm) apart; it's the finest one you're likely to find.

Pour glue onto the ground and move the blob around the entire surface with the trowel, as shown in photo 10. Regulate the glue density by adjusting the angle at which you hold the trowel.

**Photo 10**

**53**

If the trowel is held perpendicular to the ground, the spread will be maximized. Holding the trowel at a 30° to 45° angle will be about right for the glues mentioned above. Use a light spread for closed-grain woods and a heavier spread for open-grained woods. For the fruit bowl I made on page 94, it took 2.5 fluid ounces (75 mL) of yellow glue to spread the 9 x 12-inch (22.9 x 30.5 cm) ground. To shorten press time, I often work the glue for several minutes, allowing it to dry slightly. (I only do this when I will be able to load the press quickly.) Make sure all of the ridges left by the trowel are uniform in size, and don't get excited if the ridges disappear quickly. You have used the proper amount of glue—the ridges are just flowing out.

Just because the trowel is sold as a *disposable* doesn't mean you can't wash and reuse it. It's a good idea to have a brush on hand to clean between the teeth. Trowels do wear, especially the plastic ones, so keep a close eye on the teeth. As the teeth wear down, keep the tip of the trowel more perpendicular. When they are worn down about a third, dispose of the trowel.

## BRUSHES

A brush will work well for contact cement and hot hide glue, and I recommend a brush for spreading thinned glues (see the Dry Glue process on page 58). Small brushes can be used for spreading CA, provided you have a container of acetone or lacquer thinner handy to clean the brush immediately after use.

Stay away from cheap disposable brushes—even for contact cement. They tend to shed hairs that have to be picked from the glued surface. Buy good brushes and clean them after use. In the case of hot hide glue, I squeeze all of the glue I can from the brush and let it dry. It does turn rock hard, but soaking it for a couple of hours in cold water softens it.

In the case of contact cement, I leave the brush in the can and keep it tightly sealed between uses (photo 11). That's right. I use an empty gallon (3.8 L) can from the paint store and keep no more than a quart (.95 L) of contact cement in the bottom, along with the brush. (If you can't find a brush short enough for the can, cut a little off the handle). As I use the glue, I replenish it from another can.

*Photo 11*

If you try my trick, keep the rim of the can clean so it will seal tightly between uses. If some hardened glue forms in the rim, fill it with lacquer thinner, replace the lid gently, and let the rim and lid soak for 15 minutes or so. Then remove the lid and clean it and the rim with the brush. Don't be tempted to poke holes in the rim so the glue will flow back into the can. If you do, the soaking trick won't work.

## ROLLERS

A paint roller works for spreading glues. However, uniformity is harder to maintain, cleanup is much more involved, and there's a lot of glue wasted in just soaking up the roller. I do use a roller to spread contact cement, but I also leave it in the can to avoid the need for cleanup.

# METHODS OF BONDING

Now that we've selected our veneers, learned how to cut them, chosen a ground, and investigated adhesives, it's time to bond the pro-ject. We can bond each piece separately or tape all of the pieces together and bond the project as a unit. Different projects call for different approaches, just as different adhesives call for different bonding techniques.

## HAMMERING WITH HOT HIDE GLUE

I recommend this method only for bonding pattern-cut pieces one at a time. This is not the bonding method to use for a taped-up project.

You don't actually hit anything with a veneer hammer. And, it's not really a hammer at all. It's a stout squeegee used to press the veneer into the hot glue. I don't own a real veneer hammer (and I do a lot of veneering with hot hide glue). I have a *home brew*, shown in the top of photo 1. For most marquetry projects with small and medium pieces, I use an automobile window scraper, seen in the lower part of photo 1. It works great and is a fraction of the cost of a veneer hammer.

**Photo 1**

To begin the hammering process, first spread the hot glue onto the ground with a brush, as shown in photo 2. (See page 48 for glue preparation.) Spread only the area that will receive the piece to be bonded. Next, position the veneer on the hot glue and work the excess to the edges with the squeegee, as shown in photo 3, while forcing the veneer into tight contact with the ground.

If you're working in a cool area, or if it's going to take a while to set your veneer in place, you'll want to keep the glue fluid longer, because once the glue congeals, you can't squeegee it to the edges. To extend your *open time* preheat your ground by wrapping it in an electric blanket or placing it in a warm oven for a few minutes.

Once the veneer is placed in the glue, the combination of warmth and moisture will cause the veneer to curl up around the edges. To prevent this, either wet the face of the veneer, or spread a small amount of glue on the face to equalize the moisture. I prefer to spread glue on the face, since this also provides a lubricant for the squeegee and does not dry as quickly as plain water. Any glue that is not pulled off the surface with the squeegee can be easily sanded off when completely dry.

**Photo 2**

**Photo 3**

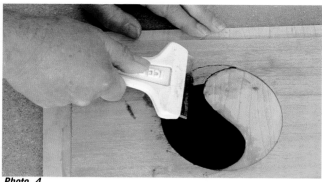

Photo 4

Photo 5

Photo 6

Once the first piece has set for a few minutes, the second can be installed. See photo 4.

All joints bonded with hot hide glue should be allowed to set for 15 minutes or so, then taped with solid veneer tape. Don't just moisten the back of the tape; dip it in water as shown in photo 5. This will expand the paper. The tape will dry and shrink before the hide glue, which will tend to pull the joints tight. If you don't tape the joints, the veneer will dry and begin to shrink before the glue has a firm hold and the joints will tend to open.

Nothing is irreversible when bonding with hot hide glue. Even days or months after it dries—heating and wetting the area can reactivate it. Pieces may be removed, replaced, or adjusted. And, any loose spots detected days later may be put down with a little heat and moisture.

Hot hide glue is also a very effective gap filler. Glue that has squeezed up through an imperfect joint will dry to an amber color. This can make slight defects disappear. The glue will shrink in the defect as it dries, but in the sanding process, you will probably sand down to the glue. If not, you can add a little glue to the defect.

Congealed glue is easily cleaned up with a scraper or putty knife. See photo 6. If it's not contaminated with wood fibers, I return it to the pot. Glue on your hands (or tools) is not so easy to clean. As it congeals, it sticks very well and leaves hands firmly bonded to tools or whatever. Unlike CA, the release agent for hide glue does not require a complex chemical formula. Simple, warm di-hydrogen monoxide works best—that's warm water for you non-chemists. When using hot hide glue, keep a bucket of warm water and a wash cloth nearby.

# HAMMERING WITH YELLOW GLUE

This process is very effective for small pieces or very small (2 x 2 inch {5.1 x 5.1 cm}) projects.

First, spread a thin coat of yellow glue on the ground in the area that will receive the component. Position the piece or component on the ground and squeegee out the excess glue. At the same time, transfer some glue to the veneer. Then, lift the component off the ground and let the glue *tack up* or dry slightly. Before the glue turns transparent, replace the veneer and squeegee again. Should the veneer curl, simply moisten the face of the veneer. Don't forget to tape your joints, as shown in photo 5.

Be sure to clean any glue from the veneer surface before it sets. Remember that yellow glue seals veneers. Glue that has set can be sanded off, but warm water and a cloth (before it sets) is much easier. (White glue may also be hammered, but not as easily.)

# PRESSING

An extremely effective method of bonding a large, taped-up marquetry project to a ground is to use a press coupled with any of the adhesives discussed except hot hide glue and contact cement. Press bonding is quicker than one-piece-at-a-time methods. A press is just two flat plates between which the veneer and ground are placed. The plates are held tightly together with evenly distributed pressure until the adhesive dries or at least sets. The plates of a press can be made with a couple of flat pieces of ¾-inch-thick (1.9 cm) plywood, particleboard, MDF, or what-have-you. Clamps placed around the edges will hold the plates tightly together. If cost is a concern, bolts will do the job of clamps.

If your press is to be much more than 10 inches (25.4 cm) square, you will have to provide pressure in the center of the plates. Press screws specifically designed for the purpose can be mounted in wooden frames. A much more economical approach is to use a deep-reach clamp like the one shown in photo 7.

If the project is quite large, a deep-reach clamp can be impractical. In this situation, I use lumberyard 2 x 4s placed in pairs, one below and one above the press plates. See photo 8. I cut them a little longer than the press plates and since they're rarely straight, I true one edge on a jointer. I then taper each of the upper 2 x 4s so that there is a hump of about ¹⁄₃₂-inch (.75 mm) in the center. (If you don't want to taper, glue a 1½-inch-square [3.8 cm] piece of veneer in the center, as shown in photo 9.)

Photo 7

Photo 8

Photo 9

After the veneer and ground are between the plates, I set the 2 x 4s at about 8-inch (20.3) intervals and pull the ends together with clamps. It's hard to judge sufficient clamping pressure at the edge, so I slide a piece of paper under the 2 x 4 at the end, as seen in photo 10. When the clamping pressure begins to grab the paper, I withdraw the paper and snug down the clamp a little more.

*Photo 10*

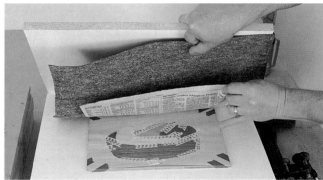

*Photo 11*

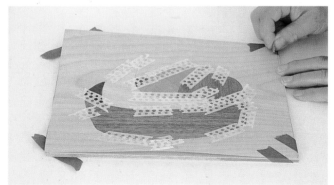

*Photo 12*

If clamps are out of your budget, there's no law against drilling the ends of the 2 x 4s and using more economical bolts, nuts, and washers. Cutting a notch in the ends of the 2 x 4s like the foreground of photo 8 will prevent the bolts from getting in the way when loading.

A marquetry project is likely to be anything but flat. If the thickness of the different veneers varies—say the thickness of a matchbook cover—great pressure will be exerted on the thicker pieces, while the thinner ones will merely float in the glue, often not bonding. Several layers of veneer tape in one area can cause the same unevenness. To remedy this, you'll need some carpet. Buy a piece of outdoor carpet, the kind that looks like heavy felt and is about $\frac{1}{8}$ inch (3 mm) thick. When placed over the veneer, this helps equalize the pressure exerted on the different thicknesses of veneer. Something should be placed between the carpet and the veneers to prevent any glue that is squeezed through the veneer from sticking to the carpet. See photo 11. Placing several layers of dry newspaper between the carpet and veneers not only prevents sticking, but draws substantial moisture from the veneers, minimizing pull. (To prevent the project from sliding on the freshly spread ground, I usually tape it in each corner as shown in photo 12.)

# DRY GLUE PROCESS

With this process, it's easier to bond the individual pieces of a project rather than a taped-up project. It's almost impossible to spread a taped-up project with glue, so when I plan to bond a taped-up project with the dry glue method, I always spread the stock before any cutting and fitting.

I mentioned earlier that the PVA glues have wonderful thermoplastic properties. Translation: they can be activated by heat. In the dry glue bonding process, both veneers and ground are spread with PVA glue and allowed to dry. Then, the two surfaces are joined and heated with a household iron. The heat reactivates (or melts) the glue and pressure from the iron helps it to adhere. When done carefully, the bond is about as strong as a wet glue bond.

One of the real advantages of the dry glue process is that pull isn't an issue. True, you're using water-based glue, and yes, the water will swell both the veneer and ground. But, before bonding occurs, the water evaporates and the materials return to their original, stable conditions. Also, heat plasticizes wood, so this process is particularly useful for applying veneers to curved surfaces. Let's take a look at this process in greater detail.

## PVA GLUES

*White Glue.* Of the PVA glues, white glue has the weakest bond, but is the easiest to use. It's reactivated at the lowest temperature—180°F (82°C). This is just below the delicate setting on most household irons.

*Yellow Glue.* A temperature of about 250°F (121°C), which is between delicate and wool, is needed for reactivation. The bond is stronger than white glue, but the surfaces need to be bonded within 7 days.

*Water-Resistant Yellow Glue.* You'll need to heat this to a temperature of 350°F (176°C)–between cotton and linen–and the surfaces should be bonded within 48 hours. Unless you're a glutton for punishment, don't use this glue for bonding. It's very hard to work with.

## SPREADING AND MISTING

No matter which you choose—white or yellow glue—use a good quality brush to spread it on both ground and veneer. Brush on two coats of glue thinned with about 10 to 20 percent water. Thin the glue to the consistency of heavy cream and allow the first coat to dry completely before applying the second. Thinned glue is easier to spread and two coats will ensure good coverage.

The moisture in the glue will cause the veneer to curl almost immediately. Prevent this by misting the face side with warm water from a spray bottle. If there is any tape on the face side of the veneer, be sure to mist very lightly. If you wet the tape too heavily, it will loosen.

## DRYING AND FLATTENING

After the veneer is glued and misted, set it on sticks (as shown in photo 13) to allow air to circulate on both sides. (Sometimes I place a fan across the room to gently circulate air over the veneers.) Also, monitor the stock as it dries, since some additional misting is often required. I learned this the hard way. Once, after spreading some veneer, I went to lunch. I returned to find a couple of pieces curled up like cinnamon sticks! Need I say that the curls were firmly stuck together?

Wait until the second coat of glue is dry to the point that all the opaque areas have turned transparent. Then, place the veneers between pieces of factory-coated particleboard and put a heavy weight on top. (If you don't want to invest in coated particleboard, you can use plywood or regular particleboard. Cover it with plastic film, so the veneers won't stick.) Burls, crotches, and curly figured species can become quite wrinkled in the

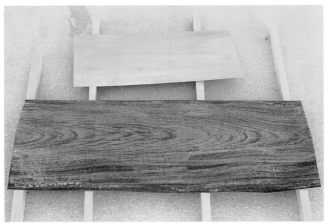

*Photo 13*

glue spreading and drying processes. If the heavy weight doesn't keep your veneers wrinkle free, add a few clamps around the particleboard.

There is generally enough residual moisture in the veneer to render it pliable. But, if any pieces feel like they may break when forced flat, heat them with a hair drier to increase pliability. The veneers should be flat within an hour.

After the glue is dry, sand both the ground and veneers lightly with a sanding block wrapped with 80-grit sandpaper. This will knock the top off any dust that may have settled in the wet glue. The veneers are now ready to be bonded.

## BONDING

Set your iron to medium high strength heat and begin to heat an area or individual piece. See photo 14. The area should be heated to a temperature that is quite warm to the touch if you used white glue, or uncomfortably warm if you used yellow glue. Keep your iron moving constantly and never let any one spot absorb the full heat. Remember, the heat must penetrate to the glue line and into the ground. The area must be kept warm long enough for the heat to soak through.

Once the area is sufficiently heated, use considerable pressure with the tip of the iron and pass it over every square inch of the piece. How much

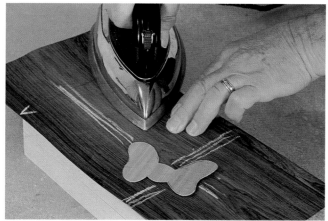

*Photo 14*

pressure is considerable? Well, I've yet to break an iron's handle, but I do recall pain in my shoulder for several days after doing a large tabletop. Lean on the iron. To meet the challenge of the different thicknesses of veneer, be very careful to pass the tip of the iron heavily over every joint, concentrating on the thinner veneers.

If your project is taped up, it will be difficult to judge where the joints are. So, after initial bonding, remove the tape by wetting and peeling it off. Wipe off any residual adhesive with a damp cloth and work on ironing the joints.

When all of the pieces are down, check the entire project for any loose spots. Move your fingernails over the project surface. Listen for any variances (suspected loose spots). Mark any loose areas with chalk and after inspecting the whole project; reheat all of the chalk marks.

As a final step, give the project the *water test* for loose spots. Wet the surface with a cloth; this will cause the veneer to swell. The spots that are not firmly bonded will pull themselves loose and talk to you with tiny clicking sounds. Also, if you can get just the right light on the project, you'll see bubbles form in loose areas. Iron these down and pass the iron over the entire surface until it's dry.

## BONDING WITH CONTACT CEMENT

I may have given the impression that I'm not fond of contact cement, and for general veneer work, that's true. However, for many marquetry projects, it's a wonderful adhesive. Contact cement is non-water-based glue, so pull is not a concern. (There are water-base contact cements, but I don't recommend them.)

As with the dry glue process, the adhesive is spread on both the ground and veneers. I usually give both two coats of full-strength contact. (Here again, I prefer to spread the veneer stock rather than the individual pieces, mostly to take advantage of the strengthening properties of the glue. While contact cement doesn't strengthen veneer as well as dry glue, it certainly helps. If I do chip off a delicate corner of stock that has been spread with contact, it usually remains attached by a string of the glue, and I don't find myself on my knees, under the bench, looking for the wayward corner and…praying.)

The contact cement on both surfaces must be dry before bonding. To check for dryness, press your finger into the glue. If the glue sticks, the contact is still too wet for bonding. Contact cement should not be overly dry before bonding and the surfaces should be joined within several hours of application. If your contact should dry out, you can reactivate it by wiping the surface with lacquer thinner. You can also respread the surfaces.

When surfaces spread with contact cement are joined, they stick immediately. This makes setting the pieces in place a bit tricky, because they must be in perfect position. So a piece got stuck that wasn't quite in the correct position? Don't panic! In these cases I use a hypodermic needle and syringe filled with lacquer thinner. See photo 15. You can free a piece by squirting the thinner under the edge and slowly and carefully lifting it. If you don't have a needle and syringe, turn your project on edge and dribble thinner under the edge of the errant piece using a spoon, eyedropper, or what-have-you.

Firmly press the veneers into the ground using a wallpaper seam roller, shown in photo 16, or veneer hammer. You could also use a block of soft-textured wood. Whatever tool you use, exert firm pressure. In many cases you will be mashing raised fibers of wood or small specks of dust in the glue line. The object is to get the surfaces into 100 percent contact.

You might encounter one little spot that just won't go down. Again, don't panic, and don't beat on it with a hammer. Heat your iron until it's uncomfortably warm to the touch. Heat the trouble spot

using the tip of the iron. The heat will make the glue more active and plasticize the wood—permitting it to easily compress. Hold the spot down with your finger until it cools.

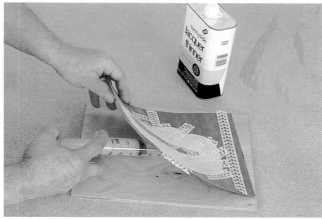

**Photo 15**

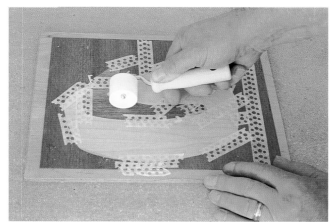

**Photo 16**

61

# FINISHING

Wood veneers are not very durable. To withstand the test of dust, moisture, air pollution, and the touch of inquisitive fingers, veneers need protection. If you've made a wall hanging, nonreflective glass in the frame might be all you need. If you've applied your project to a tabletop, a traditional wood finish might be more in order. A good finish can greatly enhance your work; it can also be more than half the job.

## OVERALL CONSIDERATIONS

You have chosen to demonstrate your art in marquetry because of the natural beauty of the medium. No paint can duplicate the subtle textures of wood, nor can it compare with the natural iridescence of wood. Perhaps you chose a particular species for its color, though the texture is not to your liking. You can deal with texture through the use of fillers, but you shouldn't do anything to interfere with iridescence.

Some marquetarians advocate endless protective coats of finish—the thicker the coating, the better. Well, I'm not one of those. My opinion is that the best finish is one that doesn't appear to be there at all. Therefore, I try to keep my finishes as thin as possible, while still providing sufficient protection.

## PREPARATION

I have always considered preparation at least 60 percent of the finishing process. No finish, especially the finishes applicable to marquetry, will hide defects, roughness, and scratches. A good finish will magnify these flaws along with the beauty of the wood veneer. That's why it's oh so important to spend time in the preparation phase. (Just like in building—an extra hour of care spent on the foundation saves ten, when it comes to framing the roof.)

## PATCHING

First, remove any and all tape. Next, inspect your project for defects. There might be a pinhole that is a little too obvious, or holes that your dividers made in the layout and cutting stage, or a joint that just isn't as tight as it should be. Yes, it happens; the joints in my work are not always perfect.

I use *nitrocellulose putty* for patching. It's economical, comes in a variety of colors, dries quickly, and sands easily. When using putty on open-grained woods, be careful to get the putty in the defect only, as shown in photo 2, since it will fill the pores of open-grained woods and often can't be sanded out.

*Photo 1*

*Photo 2*

Nitrocellulose putty doesn't always work with veneers that are likely to fade dramatically. Cherry and walnut are my most challenging. The color will be right initially, but as the veneer fades and the putty doesn't, your patches will become obvious. To prevent this, sand a scrap of the veneer that is likely to fade and collect the dust. Then, mix the dust with some thinned liquid hide glue—just enough to hold the particles of dust together—and patch. Now, the patch will fade at the same rate as the veneer.

## SANDING

Once all patches are dry, it's time to level the surface. Rarely do I resort to a machine for sanding. I find a belt sander difficult to control, although I've been using one for 40 years. One little slip, stop, or tip with a belt sander creates a lot of extra work, and there is every likelihood that you'll have another slip, stop, or tip while you're fixing the first. Random orbit sanders would seem to be the answer, but these have a soft pad under the sandpaper. A marquetry project is made from different textures of veneer, and the sander pad will cause the sandpaper to cut the softer ones more quickly than the harder. This will create an irregular surface. One sanding machine that is suitable for marquetry projects is a *stroke sander*. This machine has a belt that passes over the surface of the project and is pressed against the surface with a block that looks something like a cement-finishing trowel. These are beyond most budgets, so let's move on to something we can all afford.

To hand sand a project, start with 120-grit sandpaper wrapped around a flat block of wood. The flat block with no pad ensures that the surface will be level and all of the pieces will be sanded equally. Padding the block will cause the softer veneers to be sanded to a greater depth than the harder, producing a rippled surface.

If the grain of the veneers runs predominantly in one direction—sand with the grain, as shown in

photo 3. This is not usually the case, so we must violate the first rule of wood sanding and use a circular motion, as shown in photo 4. This circular motion, of course, leaves cross-grain scratches; fear not—these will be taken care of in phase two.

After the surface is perfectly level, switch to 180-grit sandpaper, again using the sanding block. Work with the 180-grit paper until all cross-grain scratches (left by the 120) are removed. The 180-grit paper will also leave cross-grain scratches, but these will be barely visible in many coarse veneers (oak, mahogany, ash, etc.).

**Photo 3**

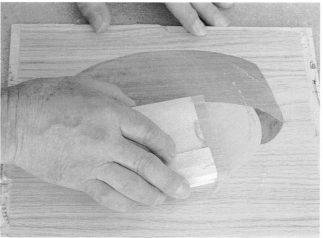

**Photo 4**

**63**

If the project has pieces of fine-grain veneers—apple, maple, pine, etc.—one final step is required. Switch to 220-grit paper and remove any cross-grain scratches left by the 180. The 220-grit paper will leave cross-grain scratches, but with few exceptions, you'll need a magnifying glass to find them. If you're inclined to get out your magnifying glass, go ahead and carry the sanding process a step or two further switching to 380-grit paper, then to 400-grit.

Between each sanding step, I brush the surface briskly, not only to eliminate dust, but to remove any traces of grit that may have fallen from the sandpaper. Particles of 120-grit that remain on the surface will continue to leave deep scratches in the 220-grit stage.

Have all of the grits of sandpaper you will need on hand. It has been said that sanding with a well-used piece of paper will produce the same effects as sanding with a finer grit. One fellow went so far as to recommend rubbing the surfaces of two sheets of 120-grit paper together to produce 220-grit paper. This doesn't work, folks. What you will be doing is sanding with a *dull* piece of the coarser grit and using a lot of extra elbow grease.

(Note: Most of the products listed below are both toxic and flammable. Be sure to read and understand all of the cautions listed on the label.)

# STAINS

When you wish to alter the overall color of a project by giving it a color cast, you'll want to use a stain. Avoid *pigmented* stains. These are color stains that come from ground pigments or *rocks*, as I call them. Pigments are not transparent, so you will be looking at your project through a film of colored mud. All or much of the iridescent properties of the veneers will be lost.

*Dye stains* are better for altering the cast of your project. These are fully transparent and will

change the cast without destroying the iridescence. Dye stains are available at hardware stores, or you could use fabric dye from the craft-supply stores. Should you choose fabric dye, omit the salt in mixing, and mix the dye with alcohol rather than water. Alcohol will dissolve most dyes and won't raise the grain of the veneers, as water will. Better still—use liquid dye concentrates mixed with alcohol.

One final word on dye staining: A *very thin* coat of bright orange, bright yellow, or a combination of the two, will enhance the colors of most all veneers. I taped off the lower half of one of the fruit bowls and sprayed the upper half with bright orange dye stain. See photo 5. Note that the upper portion of the apple and pear are more lively, and although it's very discrete, the ribbon pattern of the mahogany background is more pronounced on the stained portion.

**Photo 5**

# FILLERS

Perhaps you've used a particular veneer for its color, but you don't care for its coarse, open-grain texture. On the other hand, maybe you really like the open grain of a veneer and you want to enhance it. In both cases, the grain may be filled. To *hide* open grain, use a filler color that *matches* the surface of the veneer. To *enhance* the grain, use a *contrasting* color. If the area is small, nitrocellulose putty will work—if you can find the color you desire. For large areas, it's more economical to use a paste wood filler. This type of filler is made from finely ground sand mixed with linseed oil and a dryer agent. A wide range of colors is available, or you can tint the white paste filler. Universal tinting colors or artists oil colors are used for tinting and allow you to create any color you want. See photo 6. The color of the tinted filler can change a little in drying and topcoating, so it's a good idea to experiment with scraps and carry the process all the way through a topcoat or two.

I ignore the instructions on the can, and thin the filler to the consistency of room-temperature butter. Then, I spread it on my project, working it cross-grain into the pores. To remove the excess, I use a rubber squeegee, as shown in photo 7.

*Photo 6*

*Photo 7*

One other filler worthy of mention is hide glue. Hot hide glue works best, but the liquid type also works. Simply spread glue on the project and squeegee off the excess. The glue remains in the pores. Usually two treatments are required with overnight drying in between. The hide glue filler dries to a transparent amber color and interferes very little with the natural iridescent properties of the wood.

# OILS

The simplest type of finish I can introduce you to is an *oil finish*. Oils in general are not surface coatings, but rather penetrating finishes. For centuries, linseed oil was the product to use, but Danish oil and tung oil serve the purposes of the marquetarian in a far superior manner.

## DANISH OIL

**65**

*Danish oil* is the deepest penetrating finish I know. In most cases it will penetrate completely through veneers to the glue line. As it dries and cures, it hardens the veneers and produces a transparent effect that will enhance the iridescent properties of the wood.

Danish oil may be applied with a brush or rag. I use a piece of synthetic sponge or scrap foam rubber. See photo 8. I also wear disposable latex

*Photo 8*

gloves to protect my hands. Apply the Danish oil in a heavy, wet coat. Keep the surface wet with oil for 10 minutes, or so. Soft-textured veneers will absorb much more oil than the harder-textured, so you'll need to keep them wet longer. When dry spots have stopped forming, consider the job complete, and wipe the residual oil from the surface.

Danish oil cures through chemical reaction, and heat is produced in the curing process. This means that wet gloves, rags, foam applicators, and such left in a pile can spontaneously combust. I have several colleagues who have experienced such fires. The safest way to dispose of these items is to separate them and lay them out on a concrete floor or outdoors to dry completely. In my paint shop I have a clothesline to hang flammable rags. Once they're completely dry (usually after several days), you may dispose of them safely.

After the first application of oil, tiny beads of oil may exude from the surface of the veneer. This may go on for a day or two after the application, or at any rate, until the oil is completely dry. This is normal, and indicates that you gave the veneers a proper coat of Danish oil. Simply wipe off the spots so they won't leave gummy blobs on the surface.

Once the oil is dry, and this may take up to a week, give the project another coat of oil and sand thoroughly with 400-grit wet-or-dry sandpaper, (no block) using the oil as a lubricant. This will remove any dust from the surface and cut away any wood fibers that were raised in the first oiling. Particles removed by the sandpaper will pack into any voids in joints or open grain, leaving the surface very smooth and very level.

Wipe all oil and particles from the surface and let the project dry for several more days, then give the project a coat of paste wax, using #0000 steel wool as an applicator. See photo 9. After buffing the wax with a soft cloth, as shown in photo 10, you will have a long-lasting matte finish.

*Photo 9*

*Photo 10*

## TUNG OIL

Made from tung nuts, this oil is similar to Danish oil but is used a little differently. *Tung oil* is applied to the surface sparingly with a small piece of soft cloth. See photo 11. If you saturate the project, you might not live long enough for the oil to dry. Several coats are applied with several days in between allowed for drying. Sand lightly with 400-grit sandpaper between coats. When the desired sheen is obtained, allow at least a week before any rough handling. Tung oil is wonderful in that the type blended without dryers or solvents is nontoxic and can be used to finish items to be used around food, or handled by small children.

*Photo 11*

# SHELLAC

This product is made by dissolving resins from the carcasses of tiny bugs in alcohol, and it's been used in wood finishing for centuries. It's not nearly as durable as other topcoats, but it has great value as a sealer. *Shellac* will seal oils, resins, and dyes, and keep them from bleeding to the surface of other topcoat products. Use it as a first (or sealer) coat, let it dry, and then lightly sand the surface. This will create a smooth surface for the application of other products. Shellac is available as a liquid or as flakes that you dissolve in alcohol. The liquid has a limited shelf life (check the label), but the flakes will last indefinitely if stored in a cool, dry place. White shellac dries clear and orange shellac dries with a transparent orange cast. Orange shellac, used as a thin sealer, brightens and livens most veneers. You might want to try it, but experiment with some scrap pieces first.

# VARNISH

There are many formulations of *varnish* available. Some are brewed for special-purpose applications. You can choose from a variety of sheens, from high-gloss to dead flat (photo 12). Some are blended with an ultra violet light (UV) inhibitor—these are the greatest value to the marquetarian because they prevent your veneers from changing color.

I have several objections to varnishes of any kind and rarely use them, except for exterior applications. My main objection is the slow drying time, which ranges from an hour for the fast-drying types, to several hours for the more traditional blends. During this time, the wet surface can pick up all sorts of floating dust. (In order to have a smooth surface, that dust must then be sanded flat and the surface polished—I don't know about you, but I have better things to do.)

Some varnishes tend to turn yellow, which will alter the color of a project. Some are slightly milky, which will detract from the veneer's beautiful iridescence. Also, varnishes do not bite. That is to say, the second coat does not partially dissolve the first and flow into it. This lack of bite leaves all the coats in separate layers. For a project that demands maximum durability (for instance, a decorated tabletop) this can be problematic. A hot beverage cup can cause separation of the layers and leave a cloudy white spot.

# LACQUER

My all-time favorite topcoat is *lacquer* (photo 13). Lacquer should be applied with spray equipment, in a spray booth. If this is beyond your reach, you can purchase lacquer in aerosol cans. (Only use this product in a well-ventilated area, free from

*Photo 12*

*Photo 13*

any source of combustion.) Lacquer comes in different sheens and dries in a matter of seconds, so there are no dust problems. Lacquer also bites and is extremely durable. *Lacquer sanding sealer* is available in aerosol form, too. This is used as a first (and second) coat to seal the work. It sands easily and does not clog sandpaper. It leaves a smooth, level surface for the lacquer topcoats (two or three should be sufficient).

There are brushing-type lacquers and sanding sealers. These may be applied with a conventional or foam brush. Brushing lacquers are every bit as durable as spraying lacquers, but because they dry very quickly, they must be spread very quickly. Allow plenty of drying time between coats. Brushing lacquers bite, so don't apply a second coat until the first is completely dry.

## DEFT

One product that has some of the brushing characteristics of varnish and the drying properties of lacquer is *Clear Liquid Deft* (photo 14). It can be used as its own sanding sealer, and it dries to the touch in about 15 minutes, minimizing the dust challenge. It dries to recoat in about two hours. Let it dry overnight, and it may be sanded between coats without clogging no-fill sandpaper. Successive coats do bite somewhat, creating a continuous film protection.

Photo 14

## WATER-BASED COATINGS

If you live in an area that has outlawed the use of solvent-based chemical coatings, you will use a water-based topcoat (photo 15). I used to advise taking a project across the border for finishing, but in recent years I've softened my attitude, because great strides have been made in this industry. Some of the water-based coatings are even more durable than those I've listed above, and some are completely nontoxic, though I wouldn't recommend a taste test. While these coatings do not bite, some do dry dust-free in as little as 20 minutes—a definite plus. On the minus side, these coatings tend to be somewhat milky if applied too thick. But if you take my advice on finishes (less is more), this won't be a problem.

Photo 15

## RUBBING AND POLISHING

You may wish to carry your finish to the max and polish the surface. If you have ornamented a tabletop, a tray, or a fine piece of furniture, this is highly recommended.

The first step in the process is wet sanding. This should not be undertaken before the last coat has had a chance to thoroughly cure—several days. I use a circular motion with hand-held 400-grit wet-or-dry sandpaper, folded in thirds. See photo 16. The sandpaper requires a lubricant to keep it from clogging. Water will work, but soapy water works even better. Use about ½ teaspoon (.25 mL) of

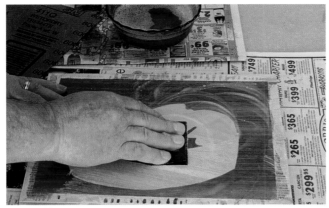

Photo 16

dish-washing liquid per quart (.95 L) of water. You can also use mineral oil or baby oil.

First, you want to level the surface: sand out any dust particles, brush marks, or overspray. Continually check the sandpaper to make sure it's not clogging. The tiniest clog can scratch deeply. Once the surface is level, clean it to remove any finish particles, and more important, any sandpaper grit. At this point the surface of your project will look quite dull.

For the next round of sanding, use 600-grit wet-or-dry sandpaper. The intent is to remove all the scratches left by the 400-grit. I can usually tell when I've reached my goal because the 600-grit paper will tend to grab and slip from my hand. At this point, I clean the surface again.

We're in the homestretch now; polishing is all that remains. For a satin finish, polish with #0000 steel wool and a lubricant—soap and water, baby oil, what-have-you. For a higher sheen, the traditional method is to use powered pumice followed by *rottenstone*. I've used these products, and they work well. As I've grown lazy in my advanced years, I use *rubbing compound* and *swirl mark remover* (also called *final finish* or *topping*) available at your local auto parts store. The rubbing compound is a liquid product that comes in several grits. I've found the fine works best. I apply some of the liquid rubbing compound to a rag folded into a pad. I pass it firmly over the surface of the project, as shown in photo 17. I dribble a few blobs on the project so I can pick up fresh rubbing compound

as I work. After the rubbing compound dulls and begins to clog the pad, I turn the pad and apply more liquid. After several changes, I begin to wish that the auto parts store also sold elbow grease and perspiration remover.

Now, I clean the surface and apply the swirl mark remover, as shown in photo 18. This product contains a tiny bit of very fine grit and something similar to wax, which will remain on the surface. I apply it sparingly with a rag, and after it dries slightly, I buff vigorously with a dry, soft cloth.

Ta, da, the result is a highly polished finish. (See photo 19.)

Photo 17

Photo 18

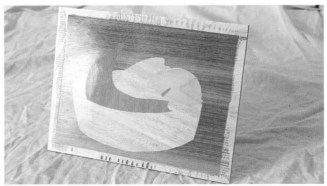

Photo 19

# GALLERY
## MARQUETRY

GALLERY

**Paul R. Dean,** *Rick Hanson.*
Photo by artist

**Frank Helvey,** *Louisiana Blue Heron.* Flat cut
maple background with dyed blues and greens,
walnut, ebony, poplar, holly, and rosewood .
Photo by Edward Reilly

**Frank Helvey,** *Nap Time on the Serengeti.* Maple, walnut
crotch, satinwood, dyed black and dark pearwood.
Photo by Edward Reilly

**Claude Edwards,** *Praying Hands.* Cherry, mahogany, maple, curly maple, walnut, rosewood, primavera. Photo by artist

**Michael Gaide,** *Penguins.* Photo by artist

**Claude Edwards,** *Hatteras Lighthouse.* Cherry, butternut, mahogany, maple, walnut. Photo by Claudia Page

**Hanya Kandlis,** *As Above So Below.* Quarter-sawn blown oak, quilted maple, redwood burl, holly, ash, mother-or-pearl, silver, ruby. Photo by Rob Ratkowski

**Hanya Kandlis,** *Lady on the Bridge.* Walnut crotch, oak, holly, carpathian elm burl, dyed holly, mahogany, ash, mother-of-pearl. Photo by Rob Ratkowski

**Michael Gaide,** *Vase with Chrysanthemum.* Photo by artist

**GALLERY**

**T. Breeze Verdant,** *Magnolia Table.* Photo by Tom Raffelt

**Michael Gaide,** *The Forgotten Message (detail).* Photo by artist

**Michael Gaide,** *Morning Glory.* Photo by artist

GALLERY

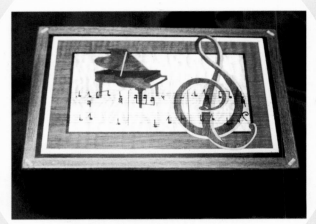

**Ray Wisner,** *Music Box.* Photo by artist

**Michael Gaide,** *Bamboo.* Photo by artist

**Michael Gaide,** *Tracks.* Photo by artist

GALLERY

# MARQUETRY
# PROJECTS

*T*he following projects will allow you to practice your newly acquired skills and techniques. Refer back to the earlier technical information to refresh your memory and confirm your understanding of methods and procedures. And feel free to alter any of the projects to fit your particular needs and desires. You can use $^{1}/_{4}$-inch (6 mm) MDF ground for all of the projects, or apply the projects to other objects.

# CD Cabinet

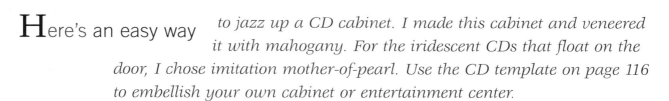

Designed by Mike Burton

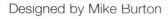

Here's an easy way *to jazz up a CD cabinet. I made this cabinet and veneered it with mahogany. For the iridescent CDs that float on the door, I chose imitation mother-of-pearl. Use the CD template on page 116 to embellish your own cabinet or entertainment center.*

**1**— Carefully examine your zebra wood. Select three areas with five distinct, dark lines. Cut out these three strips parallel with the dark lines, but leave some lighter wood at the top and bottom. The length will depend on the size of the cabinet to which you're applying the marquetry.

**2**— Inlay these three pieces into the mahogany background. Tape them in place securely.

**3**— Layout, cut, and fit the black poplar notes, as desired. If you read music, pick a tune.

**4**— Do not cut the stems of the notes yet. These will be inlayed after bonding. Use stabbing cuts to cut those tiny notes. (Note: A small gouge blade for your hobby knife will make cutting the notes a snap. To cut the window, make two punching cuts, end-to-end. Do the same to cut the black poplar to fit into each.)

5 — Cut and fit bars to tie some of the notes together.

6 — You've probably noticed that the mother-of-pearl is about twice as thick as the mahogany. So, bond the background, notes, and staffs to another sheet of mahogany with the grain running perpendicular to the grain of the background.

7 — Bond two thicknesses of 2-inch-square (5 cm) butternut and two thicknesses of 2-inch-square (5 cm) mahogany together for the center portions of the CDs.

8 — Mark the mother-of-pearl using the CD pattern supplied and transfer paper. Carbon paper will smear easily on the smooth surface. Cut the CDs from the mother-of-pearl using your fret saw.

9 — Cut a window in the center of the CD to receive a double thickness of butternut, to depict the noniridescent portion of the CD. Tape in place.

10 — Cut a window in the butternut to receive a double thickness of mahogany, (to depict the hole in the CD). Tape in place.

11 — Inlay the CDs into the background. (Before taping the CDs in place, scuff the backs with 80-grit sandpaper. This will help create a strong bond.)

12 — Bond the project to the cabinet door. (Note: It's not necessary to veneer the back of the door to prevent pull. The opposing grains of the project will create sufficient stability.) Remove all the tape.

13 — Inlay the note stems. Cut a V-shaped groove at the location of each and glue in a V-shaped piece of black poplar. I highly recommend hide glue for the job. If you use *liquid* hide glue, have some weights on hand to hold the tiny pieces until the glue sets.

14 — Let the glue dry overnight. After the glue has dried, the door is ready for sanding and finishing. Consider a satin lacquer.

**Materials**
- Zebra wood (Staffs)
- Poplar dyed black (Notes and CD holes)
- Imitation mother-of-pearl (CDs)
- Butternut (CD inner circles)
- Mahogany (Background)

**83**

**Tools**
- Knife
- Fret saw with bird's mouth and #0 blade
- Veneer tape
- Drill
- Pencil
- Transfer paper
- 80-, 120-, 220-grit sandpaper
- Straightedge
- Small gouge
- Glue for bonding

## Materials

- **Gray Harewood**
- **Blue Harewood**
- **Sycamore**
- **Ebony Macassar**
- **Walnut**
- **Mahogany**
- **Iroko**
- **Temporary background or waster 9 x 10 inches (22.9 x 25.4 cm)**

## Tools

- **Your favorite knife**
- **Sand-shading equipment**
- **Veneer tape**
- **Low-tack tape**
- **Straightedge**
- **Ruler**

*(Note: Enlarge the pattern to whatever size picture you wish to create.)*

*—The designer used a limited number of veneers because with a night scene a variety of color was unnecessary. Secondly, he selected similar veneers and used the different shades in the veneers to create contrasts. Blue harewood was chosen for the sky and the lake mainly because of the minimal grain effect in the veneer. He wanted to create a smooth glasslike finish on the lake to show the reflection of the moon. He also did some sand shading around the edges of the moon and its reflections to add a three dimensional effect.*

# Rock Isle Lake

Here's a chance to *create some beautiful marquetry, lea how to develop depth in a picture, ar hone your technical skills. You'll start in the background and work your way to the foreground. Any veneers may be selected to represent night or day.*

1— Use a 9 x 10-inch (22.9 x 25.4 cm) temporary background or waster. This will be large enough to cover the top of the sky to the shoreline of the lake in front of the mountain range. Trace the lines of the sky and the top of the mountain range, leaving a 1-inch (2.5 cm) border all around the edges.

2— Now cut the pieces from the dark blue and gray harewood veneers to construct the sky. (Ignore the moon for now.) Make sure you extend over the edges of the picture into the 1-inch (2.5 cm) border so that you have something to trim when the picture is completed. Extend over the top line of the mountain too.

3— Trace the complete circle of the moon on the sky and cut the moon piece from the sycamore veneer. (You could substitute a very light piece of burr—poplar or oak—to create a moon with craters.)

4— Trace the mountains below and across the moon. Start working with the mountains at the back and move forward until the shoreline pieces are in place. Select from the harewood, ebony, walnut, mahogany, and iroko veneers for the best contrast. (To create the effect that the light from the moon is centered in the basin of the shoreline—position the darker pieces at the edge of the picture and the lighter pieces in the middle.)

85

Designed by Paul Dean

**(5)**— Use a large piece of gray harewood to cover the area between the mountain shoreline and the rocks in the foreground. Fit it to the shoreline, but leave some extra where the rocky foreground will go. Trace the moon reflections and other markings onto the lake. (Leave out the details of the island for the time being, because these will be added later.)

**(6)**— Cut and insert the pieces of the moon reflection and lake contrasts, starting at the mountain shoreline and moving forward. Sand shade the edge of the moon reflection and insert.

**(7)**— Trace the details of the island onto the lake. Cut and insert the pieces for the island. The island is made up of rocks and trees. I used ebony macassar, which has a combination of light and dark streaks for the trees. Again, start at the back of the island and insert pieces as you move to the front. For the trees, keep the grain vertical. For the rocks, keep the grain horizontal.

**(8)**— Now, work on the foreground. Notice that I used mostly ebony veneers to create a dark and rocky ledge on which the three dead trees stand.

**(9)**— Once the foreground is finished, start on the trees. Cut the central trunk first and then the branches. Start with the top branches and finish with the bottom ones. When the tree is completed, add the three other trunks.

**(10)**— Trim the edges of the picture.

## To frame the picture as shown

**(1)**—Use a thin ⅛-inch (3 mm) border of sycamore to outline the picture.

**(2)**— Cut four pieces of walnut 1-¼ inches (3.2 cm) wide. Make the lengths slightly longer than the finished picture size. (If possible, use four consecutive leaves of veneers, which should be kept the same way round.)

**(3)**— Use low-tack tape to attach the sycamore around the edges of the picture. Miter the corners by cutting across the intersecting veneers.

**(4)**— Tape the first short piece of walnut to the top of the picture, then turn the second piece over, and tape it to the bottom. This gives a symmetrical appearance to the top and bottom borders. Repeat with the side borders to create the same effect. Miter the corners and hold them together with tape.

**(5)**— Your picture is now ready for bonding and finishing.

# Purple Iris

T his colorful project *offers you the chance to try your hand at veneer dying.*
*Holly is the only veneer you need, plus a background.*
*The flower has three different shades of purple!*

Designed by Karsten Balsley

## Materials

- *Holly*
- *Background veneer (bubinga was used here)*
- *Ground material (your choice)*

## Tools

- *Tape or rubber cement*
- *Pencil*
- *Transfer paper*
- *Hobby drill*
- *Fret saw and bird's mouth*
- *#2/0 blade*
- *Alcohol-based aniline dyes*
- *Violet, very strong, medium, and diluted*
- *Yellow, standard mix*
- *Forest Green, strong mix*
- *Moss Green, standard mix*
- *Rubber gloves*
- *Glass jars*
- *Veneer tape*

*(Note: Some experimentation is needed when dying veneers; it's not an exact science. Try different mixes to create the intensity of color you desire. For lighter shades, try a variety of dilutions. Wear gloves and protect your surroundings and clothes. Use glass jars to hold your dyes.)*

**1** — Stack the holly on top of your background veneer. Tape the pieces together, or use rubber cement to hold.

**2** — Use a piece of tape to hinge your pattern to the holly. Transfer the pattern to the holly.

**3** — Drill a small hole (the same size as your blade) along an outline. Insert the blade and begin cutting out all the pieces. Take your time and cut very carefully.

**4** — Separate your pieces. Keep all the holly pieces well organized, so you will be sure to place them in the correct dye. Refer to the pattern and project photograph, if needed. Set aside the three pieces that are natural—these will not be dyed.

**5** — Place the appropriate iris and bud pieces in the three shades of violet—very strong, medium, and diluted. (Use the photograph for reference.)

— Place the three petal pieces in the yellow.

— Place the inside leaves in the moss green.

— Place the outside leaves in the forest green.

— Let the pieces sit in the dye for five to seven days.

**6** — Remove the pieces from the dye and allow them to dry thoroughly.

**7** — Fit the pieces into the background veneer and secure with veneer tape.

**8** — Your iris is now ready to be bonded. (Note: The designer used a 30-minute clear epoxy to bond this project. It fills the gaps well and creates strong black highlight lines.)

**9** — After you've bonded your project, finish as desired.

# Decorated Canisters

Designed by Mike Burton

**W**hen marquetry shows up *in an unlikely place, it's always an eye-catcher. This trio of stainless-steel canisters is embellished with wheat, sugar beet, and coffee bean designs. These would look great in any kitchen. Four stars!*

## Materials

- **Butternut for the backgrounds**
- **Mahogany**
- **Lacewood**
- **Zebra wood**
- **Walnut**
- **Ebony**
- **Cherry**
- **Cherry with sap wood**

## Tools

- **Your favorite knife**
- **24-inch (61 cm) straightedge**
- **Square or drawing triangle**
- **Pencil**
- **Transfer paper**
- **Woodburner**
- **Putty knife**
- **Brush (for spreading contact cement)**
- **Roller or soft block of wood for bonding**
- **120 and 220-grit sandpaper**

**90**

## Flour canister

①— Prepare the butternut backgrounds for all three canisters. Depending on the size of your canisters, you might have to tape several pieces together for the necessary width. Make sure you have ample material to cover each canister, but leave both the width and length oversized by at least 10 percent.

②—In the approximate center of the largest background, transfer and mark the wheat pattern.

③—Using the window-cutting method, cut and insert the zebra wood pieces. (You don't have to be absolutely precise in the areas where the lacewood will be inserted.) Tape in place.

④—Now, cut out the lacewood pieces. Fit in place and tape.

⑤—Next, cut and fit the cherry and cherry sap depicting the twisting *blades*. Tape in place.

⑥—Finally add the cherry *stems* and secure with tape.

## Sugar Canister

①—In the approximate center of the medium-size background, transfer and mark the sugar beet pattern.

②—Cut and insert the mahogany body first. (Running the grain of the mahogany across the beet looks most realistic.) Tape in place.

③—Continue by cutting, inserting, and taping the leaves. (Note the grain change at the center of each leaf.)

④—Shade the upper edge of the lower piece of the right leaf with the woodburner. This will enhance the curling effect. Insert this piece.

⑤—Finally cut and fit the cherry sap wood stems. Tape to hold.

# Coffee Canister

**1** — In the approximate center of the smallest-size background, transfer and mark the coffee bean pattern.

**2** — Cut and insert the beans in the foreground first. Tape to secure.

**3** — Cut out the background beans next. Heat shade the edges of any background beans that join the foreground beans.

**4** — Insert the beans and hold with tape.

**5** — Cut and insert the cherry highlight.

**6** — Finish by cutting and inserting the stems and tiny pieces of ebony depicting the flower ends of the beans. Tape all securely to hold.

**7** — If the veneers become distorted from the drying tape, moisten the back of the assembly (the side opposite the tape) and iron it flat.

**8** — Use a straightedge to trim the edges of each taped-up assembly, so each fits the exact height of the canisters.

**9** — Use a square or drawing triangle to square one end of each assembly and wrap it around the appropriate canister. Mark the seam in the back.

**10** — Cut the seams. Be *exact*. (If you cut a little long—about the thickness of a matchbook cover—that's OK.)

**11** — Spread both veneers and canisters with two coats of contact cement, allowing complete drying between coats.

**12** — After the second coat of contact has dried, stand the veneer on end and slide the canister into its center. Once the glue grabs at the center

point, carefully work the veneer around the canister. Use only moderate pressure to bond the piece at this time.

**13** — If, at any time, the veneer seems to be going awry, STOP. Dribble some lacquer thinner on the contact cement to release it, let everything dry and try it again.

**14** — Bond one end completely, but stop about 2 inches (5 cm) short with the other. If the veneer is slightly long, buckle this 2 inches (5 cm) and make the joint first. (If the veneer is a tiny bit short, it can be stretched slightly.)

**15** — Once the veneer is in place, turn the canister on its side and apply firm pressure with a roller, veneer hammer, block of soft wood, or what-have you. (If the bottoms of your canisters are rounded, like mine, avoid bonding pressure near this area.)

**91**

**16** — Mix either epoxy or auto-body putty and fill the void between the rounded bottom of the canister and the veneer. Fill the void completely. If the filler stands a bit proud of the void much the better. Once the filler has dried, sand it flush with the bottom of the canister.

**17** — Slightly round off the edge of the veneer with sandpaper so it won't catch on anything and be chipped.

**18** — The canisters are now ready for sanding and finishing.

Designed by Gary White

# Ohio Stars Box

## Materials

- Wenge
- Narra
- Maple

(If you choose to make a wall hanging—¼ inch [6 mm] MDF ground material.)

## Tools

- Your favorite knife
- Transfer paper
- Veneer tape
- Glue for bonding
- Clear lacquer and finishing supplies

A classic quilt design *graces the lid of this handmade box. Each star is made from 32 triangular pieces. The symmetry of the design is complemented by the direction of the veneer's grain. You can apply this design to anything you fancy—a tray, cabinet door, chest, or your favorite box top. You can also make a wall hanging, or use this as a border design.*

**1** — Enlarge the pattern to create the appropriately-sized design to fit your particular needs.

**2** — Transfer the design onto a background veneer or waster (temporary background).

**3** — You will be cutting many sharply pointed pieces, and chances are you'll experience some chipping or tearing. Before you do any cutting, consider strengthening your veneers by sizing them or making your own paper-back.

**4** — Use the window cutting method to cut out the pieces. As you replace the windows with contrasting veneers, secure the pieces in place with veneer tape.

**5** — Pay close attention to the direction of the grain. Follow the arrows on the pattern.

**6** — Once you have all the windows filled, bond your project.

**7** — To enhance the natural beauty of the veneers, finish with a clear lacquer. Then, hand polish with oil and wax.

**93**

# Fruit Bowl

**M**any fine artists use *this classic study—a bowl of fruit. This is a good beginning project, because there aren't many pieces and the pieces are large. There are a couple of tight cuts to challenge you, along with some shading and highlighting.*

Designed by Mike Burton

**1** — Hinge the pattern to the oak background veneer with tape.

**2** — Transfer the pattern with transfer or carbon paper.

**3** — Draw or cut a straight line from one tip of the bowl to the other.

**4** — Finish cutting out the rest of the bowl window. Cut the walnut bowl to fit the window. It is not necessary to fit perfectly to the straight line, since other windows will be cut in this area.

**5** — Tape the walnut veneer into the bowl window.

**6** — Transfer the design for the mahogany apple and cut the window. Again, it's not necessary to critically fit the left-hand side of the apple. Windows will be cut into this area for the pear and banana.

**7** — Cut out the apple and tape it into the window.

**8** — Continue in this manner with the pear, the two inside bowl pieces, and the end of the banana.

**9** — Bond the project using your favorite method.

**10** — Remove all of the tape.

**11** — Sand the project with 120-grit sandpaper to level all of the veneers. It's not necessary to final sand at this time.

**12** — Apply chlorine bleach using a cotton swab to highlight the area around the top of the apple.

**13** — While the bleach is working, use your wood burner to define the apple stem and the shadow around the stem.

**14** — Add a little shade with your woodburner at the stem of the pear.

**15** — After the bleach has worked (about an hour), wipe the area with vinegar to neutralize it.

**16** — Allow the project to dry.

**17** — Sand with 220-grit sandpaper, and apply your favorite finish.

Materials
- *Oak*
- *Ebony or a dark-colored burl*
- *Walnut*
- *Avodire*
- *Satinwood*
- *Mahogany*

Tools
- *Tape*
- *Your favorite knife*
- *Straightedge*
- *Woodburner*
- *Chlorine bleach*
- *Cotton swabs*
- *Pencil*
- *Transfer paper*
- *120- and 220-grit sandpaper*

**95**

# Corner Flower

**H**ere's a marquetry opportunity *to work with some materials other than veneer. You can apply this eye-catching corner pattern to your favorite box, tabletop, tray, or cabinet door. Make a mirror image of the pattern for an opposing corner design.*

Designed by Karsten Balsley

1 — Use a piece of tape to hinge your pattern to the background veneer. Transfer the pattern to your background veneer.

2 — Drill a small hole (the same size as your blade) in the center of each flower.

3 — Cut out the petals and use the cutouts to trace the petal patterns onto the tulipwood. Use a fine point pencil.

4 — Cut out the tulipwood petals and fit them into the background veneer. If the fit is tight, adjust your cuts. If the fit is too loose, recut. Be patient, and don't try to force the pieces into place.

5 — Continue cutting out the background veneer and using your cutouts as patterns for the rest of the design.

6 — Use small pieces of veneer tape to hold the pieces securely in place.

7 — Once you have all the pieces secured in place, bond your project to whatever surface you've chosen.

8 — Sand your design to make it level and smooth.

9 — Drill a hole the same size and depth as your paua shell dot for the center of each flower.

10 — Glue the shell dots into place.

11 — Finish your project as you like.

## Materials

- Paua shell or mother-of-pearl
- Tulipwood
- Copper
- Nickel silver
- Ironwood
- Walnut
- Blackwood

## Tools

- Hobby drill
- Fret saw and bird's mouth
- #2/0 blade
- Pencil
- Transfer paper
- Veneer tape
- 120- and 220-grit sandpaper

97

(Note: The designer suggests using a jeweler's visor to magnify the cutting area. For small, intricate work, he also likes to use a good spot lamp.)

# Welcome Sign

A welcome sign is a *wonderfully inviting addition to any entry. This sign is bonded to an oversize piece of $^{1}/_{4}$-inch (6 mm) faced MDF, which was then trimmed to fit the veneers. The finish is clear lacquer. I fastened mine to the door with silicone caulking.*

Designed by Mike Burton

**1** — Select a piece of maple of ample size for the inner triangle and secure the pattern to it with a hinge of tape.

**2** — Cut a window in the maple for the largest section of the bird.

**3** — Insert a piece of lacewood with a small ray pattern.

**4** — Cut the breast, tail, and top of the head windows. Select and insert pieces of smaller-patterned lacewood. The pattern in the tail should run at about a 45° angle to the pattern in the body. The pattern in the head should run at right angles to the body. The pattern of the breast should be not quite parallel to the body.

**5** — Cut the back and remainder of the head from large ray areas of the lacewood. Insert.

6 — Cut and insert the ebony eye and bill. Keep the grain running the length of the bill.

7 — Cut and insert the walnut legs and feet. Cut the legs and feet in three pieces with the grain running the length of each.

8 — Make sure all of the components are secure with tape, and set the piece aside.

9 — Select and cut three pieces of avodire for the large triangular border. These should be oversized for easy handling and can be trimmed later. The grain of these pieces should run parallel with the sides of the triangle and join at the points.

10 — Glue a piece of walnut to the back of the lower border piece with rubber cement. This will become the letters. The grain should run *perpendicular* to the avodire, so you may have to use several pieces of walnut.

11 — Rubber cement pieces of walnut to both ends of the back lower border piece. These will become the squiggles. The grain should run *parallel* with the avodire.

12 — After the rubber cement is firmly set, *bevel cut* the welcome letters and squiggles with the fret saw.

13 — Cut the embellishments for the side borders in the same manner.

14 — Trim the maple triangle to size and fit the border pieces to it. Tape all the pieces in place.

15 — With the border pieces in place, cut a window at the apex of the triangle and insert the walnut teardrop.

16 — The piece is now ready to be bonded. Finish as desired.

Materials
- *Maple*
- *Ebony*
- *Walnut*
- *Lacewood*
- *Ribbon mahogany*
- *Avodire*

Tools
- *Your favorite knife*
- *Fret saw and bird'smouth (along with wedges to tip it for bevel cutting)*
- *Pencil*
- *Transfer paper*
- *Veneer tape*
- *Rubber cement*
- *120- and 220-grit sandpaper*

**99**

Designed by Gary White

# Carpenter's Wheel Box

Here's another classic *quilt design. The wheel pattern uses 80 pieces of contrasting veneers. Of course, you can apply the design to anything you want. How about a sewing box, blanket chest, or quilt rack?*

1 — Enlarge the pattern to create the appropriately-sized design to fit your particular needs.

2 — Transfer the design onto a background veneer or waster (temporary background).

3 — You will be cutting many sharply pointed pieces, and chances are you'll experience some chipping or tearing. Before you do any cutting, consider strengthening your veneers by sizing them or making your own paper-back.

4 — Use the window-cutting method to cut out the pieces. As you replace the windows with contrasting veneers, secure the pieces in place with veneer tape.

5 — Pay close attention to the direction of the grain. Follow the arrows on the pattern.

6 — Once you have all the windows filled, bond your project.

7 — To enhance the natural beauty of the veneers, finish with a clear lacquer. Then, hand polish with oil and wax.

## Materials
- Wenge
- Maple
- Padauk
- Cherry
- Angico
- Walnut
- ¼-inch [6 mm] MDF ground material (if you choose to make a wall hanging)

**101**

## Tools
- Your favorite knife
- Transfer paper
- Veneer tape
- Glue for bonding
- Clear lacquer and finishing supplies

# Gift Wrapped Box

$A$nybody can wrap a gift *with paper and ribbon, but why not use a permanent wrapping for years of enjoyment? From my stock of leftover veneers, I chose Brazilian rosewood and satinwood.*

Materials -Brazilian rosewoo
-Satinwood

Tools -Your favorite knife
-French curve
-Straightedge
-Veneer saw
-Iron
-White glue
-Measuring spoons
-Mister bottle and wate
-Brush
(for spreading glue)
-Transfer paper
-Woodburner or
soldering iron

This project is cut using the inlay or reverse window technique and bonded using the dry-glue process.

1 — Measure your box to determine the (approximate) sizes of veneers needed to cover.

2 — Select your veneers. The piece for the top should be wide enough to cover the width of the box without joints, and it should be long enough to cover the ends. Keep this piece intact. You'll see why as we go along. If you have a single piece of satinwood large enough for all of the ribbons and bow, keep it intact. Don't cut anything yet.

3 — Spread the veneers and box with thinned white glue. This particular box (6 x 8.5 x 2.5 inches [15.2 x 21.6 x 6.4 cm]) required 6 tablespoons (90 mL) glue and 1 $\frac{1}{2}$ tablespoons (22.5 mL) of water. (If needed, mist the face side of the veneer with water to prevent curling.)

4 — After the glue has dried, give all a second coat.

5 — Use the transfer paper to trace the bow onto the satinwood.

6 — Use your favorite knife and cut out the bow. Satinwood is rather difficult to cut, so you might want to use a guide, such as a plastic French curve, for the first couple of passes. Once the path of the knife has been established, set the guide aside and finish the cut.

Designed by Mike Burton

**7** — Center the veneer you've chosen for the top and sides of your box on the top. Tack it in place by bonding about 1 square inch (2.5 cm) at all four corners with a medium warm iron. Since the contrasting components will be inlayed later, the veneer cannot be fully bonded now.

**8** — Turn the box over and (using the box itself as a guide) trim the overhanging ends with a veneer saw. Set these aside. These will be used to cover the ends, which will make the grain pattern appear to flow around. Trim the sides in the same manner.

**9** — Hold the bow firmly in position (however you wish) and mark about one quarter of it with the tip of a knife. Make a couple of passes to establish the path of the knife. Cut only this part, and remove a section of the rosewood from within the center of the bow area.

**10** — Reposition the bow, hold it firmly in the removed area, and mark another one quarter. Remove a second section of rosewood, and replace the bow. You'll find that each time a section of rosewood is removed, the bow is easier to hold in position. Continue cutting in this manner until all of the rosewood has been removed in the bow area.

**11** — Cut the bow, releasing the portion that will represent the knot.

**12** — Use a woodburner or soldering iron to heat shade both pieces of the bow in the area that will join the knot. (Hot sand will stick to the warmed glue, and a torch could burn the glue.)

**13** — Bond the pieces of bow to the box.

**14** — With a veneer saw and straightedge, cut strips of satinwood for the ribbon. Inlay these into the rosewood.

**15** — Heat-shade the ribbon ends where they meet the bow with a wood burner or soldering iron.

**16** — Bond the pieces of ribbon along with the unbonded areas of rosewood. Turn the box over and trim any overhanging ribbon, again using a veneer saw with the box as a guide.

**17** — To tidy up the edges, use a sanding block with 120-grit paper and sand the veneers flush with the box, then run a tiny bead of white glue on the edge of the veneers. Spread it out with your fingertip and let it dry.

**18** — Bond both cover veneer (rosewood) and ribbon (satinwood) to the sides of the box as if they were one piece. For the moment, forget there is a box and a lid. Make sure the grains of the sides and top pieces line up perfectly. It should appear that the grain flows across the top and down the ends.

**19** — After bonding, tidy up each side as described in step 17. Once a side is complete, cut the veneers *exactly* at the break for the lid. Use a straightedge and veneer saw or knife. Repeat with the other side. Work only one side of the box at a time.

**20** — After you've bonded the entire box, open it and carefully sand the veneers flush with the wood of the box. Sand from the veneer toward the center of the box to prevent tearing slivers from the veneer.

**21** — The box is now ready for finishing. (You may also add a decorative lining if you wish.)

# Fly Fisherman

This design uses just two veneers—blackwood and wenge. It's pad-cut, and the ripples on the water are made from rolled silver wire inserted into the saw kerf.

Designed by Karsten Balsley

## Materials

- **Blackwood**
- **Wenge**
- **Background veneer (bubinga was used here)**
- **Silver wire**
- **Hobby drill**
- **Fret saw and bird's mouth**
- **#2/0 blade**
- **Pencil**
- **Transfer paper**

## Tools

- **Veneer tape**
- **Wire cutters**
- **Knife**

**106**

*(Note: Have your local jeweler run silver wire through their rolling mill until the wire is about 1 to 2 thousandths thinner [.002] than your saw kerf width.)*

1 — Create a pad with your background on top.

2 — Use a piece of tape to hinge your pattern to the background veneer. Transfer the pattern to your background veneer.

3 — Drill a small hole (the same size as your blade) along an outline of the fisherman. Insert your blade, and cut out the angler and his reflection. Take your time and cut very carefully.

4 — Separate your pieces.

5 — Fit the pieces into the background veneer and secure with veneer tape.

6 — Retransfer the ripples onto the new pieces.

7 — Drill a small hole (the same size as your blade) along a ripple. Insert your blade and cut out the ripples one at a time. Take your time and cut very carefully.

8 — Cut the silver to fit and press into the ripple lines.

9 — Your project is now ready to be bonded.

10 — After you've bonded your project, inlay the fishing rod. Make your cut for the rod slightly curved.

11 — Your project is now ready for finishing.

# Christmas Tree Ornaments

I've seen plenty of things *I never expected to see hanging on a Christmas tree, so why not marquetry? You can use these festive bells or any kind of holiday craft pattern. The bells are nonsymmetrical to make assembly easier.*

Designed by Mike Burton

## Materials

-3 pieces of veneer cut 4 ½ inches (11.4 cm) square each

-Mahogany, walnut, and avodire were used here

## Tools

-Fret saw and bird's mouth

-Hobby drill

-Pencil

-Transfer paper

-Veneer tape

-120- and 220-grit sandpaper

1 — Prepare two pads with one piece of each veneer. Use rubber cement to hold the three layers together. Make sure the grains run in the same direction.

2 — Transfer a bell pattern to each pad.

3 — Drill a hole at a point on the edge of the bell and insert a #3/0 or #4/0 fret saw blade. All cutting can be started from this hole with the exception of the center circle near the top of the bell. You will have to drill an additional hole here. Don't cut in from the outer edge of your veneer. (The outer veneer will end up as waste, but assembly is much easier if it is kept intact.)

4 — Cut out all of the pieces. I recommend this cutting order: Cut the triangles first, the rim of the bell next, and then the striker. As you cut the upper part of the bell, cut out the small outer circles. The inner circle can be cut as a final step. (Set the triangular pieces on the bench in the order they will be assembled— this will keep the project from becoming a puzzle.)

5 — Once all pieces are cut out, assemble three bells using contrasting pieces of veneer, as shown in the photo. Hold the pieces in place with veneer tape.

6 — Repeat steps 2 through 5 with the second stack.

7 — Bond the bells to the ¼-inch (6 mm) ground material. I taped all of the bells side by side and pressed them as a unit. (The veneers will pull the ground slightly, but it's slight, so bonding a backing veneer isn't necessary.)

8 — Once the glue is dry, remove the tape and sand all of the bells—first with 120-grit and then with 220-grit sandpaper.

9 — Cut out the bells and ground using a fret saw with a #5 blade, or use a band saw or jigsaw if you have it.

10 — Drill a small hole at the top of each bell for a hanging wire. For a finish, consider gloss lacquer. Most everything on the tree will be shiny, so why not the bells?

# Serving Tray

*T*his free-form project *allows you to get a feel for different veneers and tools, while you experiment with the different types of cuts and cutting techniques. I bonded this project with the dry glue process—so there's no need for a press and clamps. No pattern either; this is all you! Express yourself.*

Designed by Mike Burton

## Materials

-Your choice of at least 4 different species of veneer

-About 1 square foot (30.5 cm) each

-Ground material

-16 x 18 inches (40.6 x 45.7 cm) is used here

-Picture frame to fit your MDF

-Small screws

## Tools

-Knife (If you have several, try them all.)

-Straightedge

-French curve

-Scissors

-Household iron

-Brush (for spreading glue)

-Pencil

-120- and 220-grit sandpaper

-Screwdriver

*110*

(1)— Prepare both ground and veneers for the dry glue process using white glue. If you have a piece of burl in your assortment of veneers, use it for the center piece. Cut an irregular shape that will fit about a 4-inch (10.2 cm) square space. Use your favorite knife and a straightedge to make all straight cuts.

(2)— Set this piece on the ground. Secure it by heating just the center of it with the tip of an iron set medium heat.

(3)— Slide a piece of contrasting veneer about 1 inch (2.5 cm) under an unbonded edge of the first piece.

(4)— Mark the contrasting piece for cutting with a sharp pencil or the tip of your knife. Make the rest of this piece (beyond the joint area) with whatever shape pleases you. Let a French curve help you.

(5)— Tack this second piece in place. You may bond it and the first firmly where they join, but remember you will be sliding other pieces under both for marking.

(6)— Continue in this manner until you've covered your ground. After the first few pieces, challenge yourself. Make some tight-curved cuts, the kind that can only be cut with stabbing slices.

(7)— You will probably have to rough-cut some pieces, so they'll slide under the tacked pieces. If you have stout scissors, try them. If you have an assortment of knives and blades, try each. If you have a paper punch, put a few dots here and there.

(8)— If the project takes days or weeks to complete, your veneers may become harder to tack and bond. Fear not. Wipe both veneers and ground with a damp cloth, and they will bond as easily as on day one.

(9)— If some of your joints don't fit perfectly, adjust them by whittling or by sanding with an emery board. A piece of sandpaper wrapped around a pencil will work on those inside curves. Don't be *too* hard on yourself, but if you can roll a coin down an open joint, you're not being hard *enough*.

(10)— Test for loose spots and bond as needed.

(11)— As a final measure, wet the surface and iron firmly until dry.

(12)— Now for those minor imperfections:

(13)— Force white glue into any open joints, then scrape the excess from the surface with a cabinet scraper or spatula.

(14)— Sand the surface in a circular manner using 120-grit sandpaper. You will experience some clogging from the fresh glue, but as you sand, the dust is being forced into the imperfect joints and the glue is holding it. Sneaky, huh?

(15)— Once you have leveled the surface, brush it off and examine it.

(16)— If there are visible scratches from the 120-grit sandpaper, use a 220-grit until they disappear.

(17)—The tray is now ready for finishing. I clear-coated mine with lacquer.

(18)—Put your finished collage into the frame and secure it all around with small screws.

*111*

# Rocking Horse

**H**ere's a simple project *that's simply wonderful. You could apply this classic design to a toy chest, crib, or rocking chair. Of course, it would make a perfect wall hanging for any child's room. The design is made from cherry and the background is walnut, but use whatever suits your taste.*

Designed by Karsten Balsley

1 — Stack the cherry on top of the background veneer. Tape the pieces together, or use rubber cement to hold.

2 — Use a piece of tape to hinge your pattern to the cherry. Transfer the pattern to the cherry.

3 — Drill a small hole (the same size as your blade) along an outline. Insert your blade and begin cutting. Take your time, and make sure you keep your blade perpendicular to your pad.

4 — Separate your pieces.

5 — Fit the rocking horse into the background veneer and secure with veneer tape.

6 — Your project is now ready to be bonded. (Note: A 30-minute clear epoxy was used to bond this project. Notice how nicely it fills the gaps and creates the attractive black highlight line.)

7 — After you've bonded your project, it's ready for finishing.

Materials
- *Cherry*
- *Ground material (your choice)*
- *Background veneer (walnut was used here)*

Tools
- *Tape or rubber cement*
- *Pencil*
- *Transfer paper*
- *Hobby drill*
- *Fret saw and bird's mouth*
- *#2/0 blade*
- *Veneer tape*

**113**

# Yin and Yang

Designed by Mike Burton

$T$his Chinese symbol *of universal opposites is an excellent first project. There are only five pieces and no tight cuts. You can cut it with the window method, but since I bonded mine one piece at a time, I used the pattern-cutting method.*

1 —Transfer the pattern to a heavy piece of paper or poster board.

2 —Cut out all the pieces.

3 — If you want to incorporate the parallel lines, at the appropriate locations make two slits wide enough for a pencil tip to fit in.

4 —Cut out and bond the background piece.

5 —Lightly transfer the pattern of the inner pieces to the appropriate veneers.

6 —Reinforce the delicate tip areas with heavy paper tape. Transfer the patterns again over the taped areas.

7 —Cut out the pieces. Fit them into place and adjust, if needed.

8 —Bond these pieces to the ground.

9 —The set of parallel lines is optional, but if you want to include them, use the inlay method.

10 —After the inlayed lines have dried completely, the project is ready for sanding and your favorite finish.

Materials  *-Avodire*
*-Pine*
*-Black-dyed poplar*

Tools  *-Your favorite knife*
*-Pencil*
*-Transfer paper*
*-Heavy paper or poster board*
*-Heavy paper tape*
*-Straightedge*
*-120- and 220-grit sandpaper*

**115**

# Project Patterns

*Enlarge as desired.*

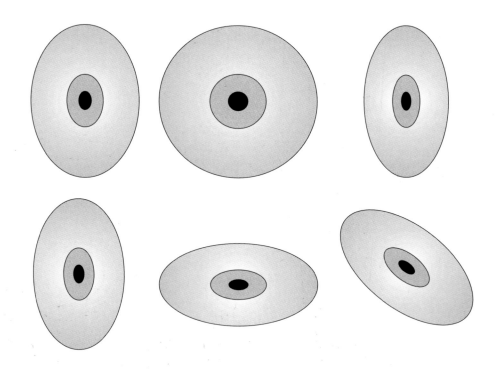

# CHRISTMAS TREE ORNAMENTS

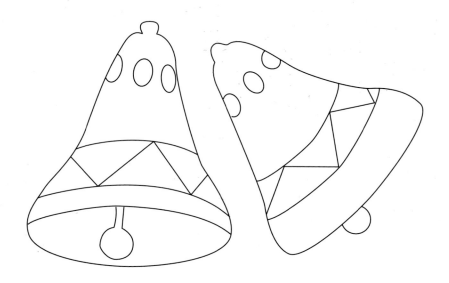

# ROCK ISLE LAKE

**1**-Hardwood gray
**2**-Hardwood blue
**3**-Sycamore
**4**-Ebony Macassar
**5**-Walnut
**6**-Mahogany
**7**-Iroko

*117*

118

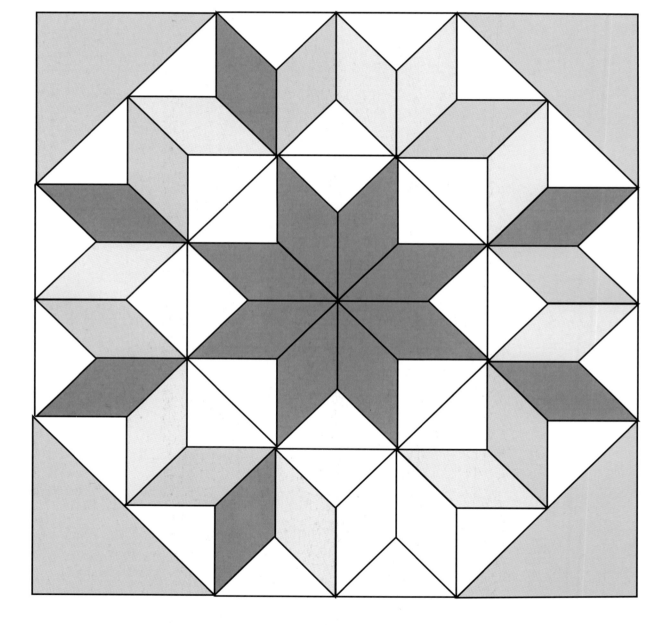

119

# GIFT WRAPPED BOX

R-Brazilian Rosewood
S-Satinwood

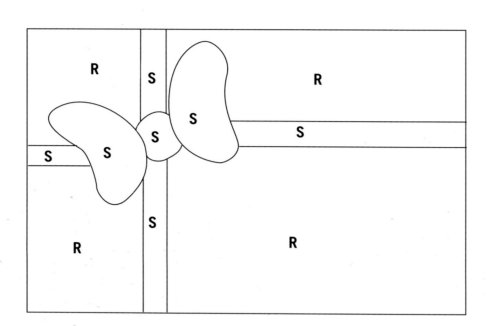

120

# YIN AND YANG

1-Avodire
2-Pine
3-Black Dyed Poplar

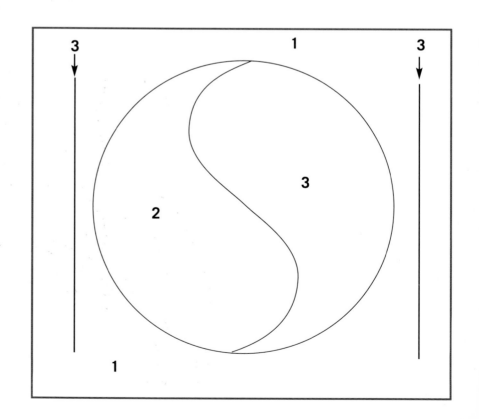

# CANISTERS

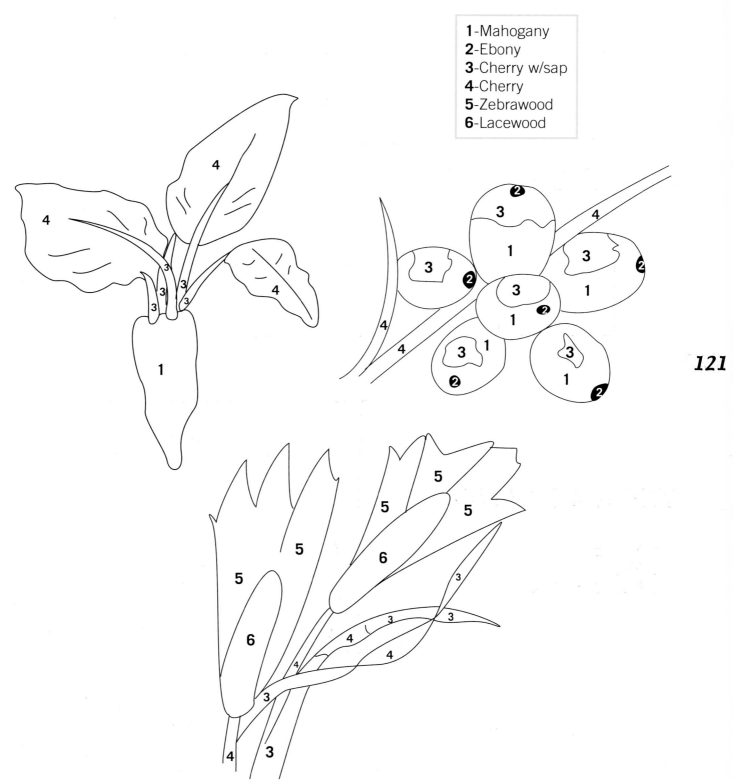

1-Mahogany
2-Ebony
3-Cherry w/sap
4-Cherry
5-Zebrawood
6-Lacewood

# WELCOME SIGN

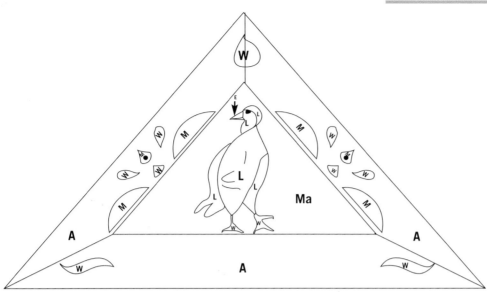

W-Walnut
A-Avodire
Ma-Maple
L-Lacewood
E-Ebony
M-Ribbon Mahogany

# FRUIT BOWL

1-Oak
2-Ebony
3-Walnut
4-Avodire
5-Satinwood
6-Mahogany

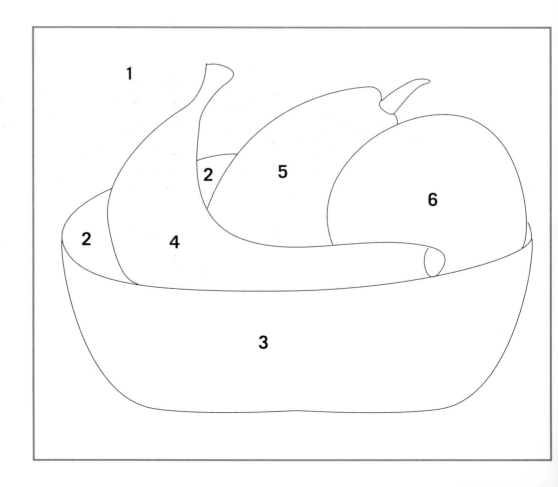

*123*

# CORNER FLOWER

1-Paua shell or Mother-of-pearl
2-Tulipwood
3-Copper
4-Nickel Silver
5-Iron wood
6-Walnut
7-Black wood

124

# PURPLE IRIS

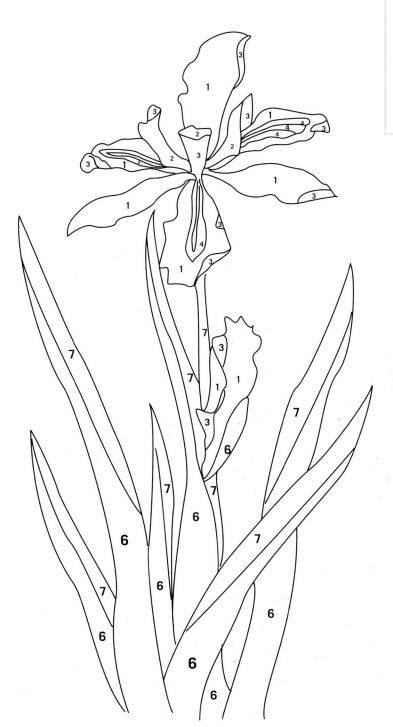

**1**-Strong violet
**2**-Medium violet
**3**-Weak violet
**4**-Yellow
**5**-Natural
**6**-Forest green
**7**-Moss green

*125*

# Contributing Marquetarians

**Karsten Balsley** has been designing and building custom furniture for over 20 years. He uses inlays and marquetry techniques on a variety of projects and specializes in custom, one-of-a-kind, and complex jobs. He works out of his one-man shop in Boulder, Colorado. Contact him at kcbalsley@worldnet.att.net.

**Paul R. Dean** lives in Calgary, and creates original marquetry pictures. He maintains an international website for the promotion of the art of marquetry at www.artmarquetry.com.

**Martin Dixon**, of Cambridgeshire, England, designs and manufactures high–quality handmade electric guitars and basses to exacting customer specifications. He may be reached at MDguitars@aol.com.

**Claude Edwards** of Winston-Salem, North Carolina, has been creating marquetry pieces for over 40 years. He makes pieces for commission, craft shows, shops, and galleries. He has also had the privilege of teaching marquetry over the years.

**Michael Gaide** lives in Osnabrueck, Germany. Before marquetry, he studied biology and worked extensively as a computer systems analyst. Michael has made his living as a professional marquetarian since 1996.

**Frank Helvey** is a retired painter and paper-hanger. He acquired a deep appreciation and knowledge of wood in his 46 years in the business. He loves the creativity of marquetry and is always looking for that one-of-a-kind piece to create.

**Hanya Kandlis** studied with a master marquetarian in Hawaii. She has enjoyed the hobby for about 10 years.

**John Russell** originally trained as a graphic designer. He has married that discipline with the art of marquetry to create unique boxes that are both beautiful and useful.

**Gary White** of Ada, Oklahoma, is a professional woodworker and maker of fine handmade boxes. His boxes are available at fine galleries throughout the United States.

**Ray Wisner** creates unique marquetry through his company Paddle Fancy in Hebron, New Hampshire. He applies his marquetry to traditional hardwood canoe paddles. Visit him at www.paddlefancy.com.

**T. Breeze Verdant** lives in Brattleboro, Vermont, where he single-handedly designs and creates his marquetry. His marquetry jewelry is available at many fine galleries throughout the United States. He also accepts commission work for furniture and boxes.

# Index